# HAUNTED
## BRIDGES

© Rich Newman

## About the Author

Rich Newman (Tennessee) has researched and explored haunted locations for more than two decades. *Haunted Bridges* is his fourth book on the subject of ghosts, and his group, Paranormal Inc., has been involved with many well-known investigations across the United States. More info regarding Rich, as well as Paranormal Inc., can be found on his website www.paranormalincorporated.com.

# HAUNTED
# BRIDGES

Over 300 of America's Creepiest Crossings

# RICH NEWMAN

Llewellyn Publications
Woodbury, Minnesota

FIRST EDITION
First Printing, 2016

Cover design: Kevin R. Brown
Cover image: iStockphoto.com/16212179/© adempercem
iStockphoto.com/60467060/© Mshake

Llewellyn Publications is a registered trademark of Llewellyn Worldwide Ltd.

**Library of Congress Cataloging-in-Publication Data**
Names: Newman, Rich, author.
Title: Haunted bridges : over 300 of America's creepiest crossings / Rich Newman.
Description: FIRST EDITION. | Woodbury : Llewellyn Worldwide, Ltd., 2016. |
   Includes bibliographical references.
Identifiers: LCCN 2016020030 (print) | LCCN 2016022779 (ebook) | ISBN
   9780738748474 | ISBN 9780738750255 (ebook)
Subjects: LCSH: Haunted places--United States. | Bridges--United States--Miscellanea.
Classification: LCC BF1472.U6 N654 2016 (print) | LCC BF1472.U6 (ebook) | DDC
   133.10973--dc23
LC record available at https://lccn.loc.gov/2016020030

Llewellyn Worldwide Ltd. does not participate in, endorse, or have any authority or responsibility concerning private business transactions between our authors and the public.

All mail addressed to the author is forwarded, but the publisher cannot, unless specifically instructed by the author, give out an address or phone number.

Any Internet references contained in this work are current at publication time, but the publisher cannot guarantee that a specific location will continue to be maintained. Please refer to the publisher's website for links to authors' websites and other sources.

Llewellyn Publications
A Division of Llewellyn Worldwide Ltd.
2143 Wooddale Drive
Woodbury, MN 55125.2989
www.llewellyn.com

Printed in the United States of America

## Other books by Rich Newman

*Devil in the Delta*

*The Ghost Hunter's Field Guide*

*Ghost Hunting for Beginners*

*For Clare, my Sugarbean*

# Contents

# INTRODUCTION

We've all heard the stories before. There's an old, spooky bridge just down the road … Or maybe it's tucked away in the countryside somewhere and is no longer in use—but if you can find it, and you can endure the darkness, you will see the scariest thing ever. It might be a ghost, it might be a mysterious light, or perhaps it's an odd voice or a cry heard in the night. But it's there. And it's waiting for you …

These are the stories that we whisper around the campfire and tell in hushed tones as we huddle in our beds just before sleep. The stories are all at once mesmerizing, unique, and familiar in an odd way. There is, of course, a good reason for this: Great scary narratives are almost always wrapped in shrouds of history and urban legend.

It would be easy to dissect many of these tales, to point out their inaccuracies, or to dismiss them outright for their lack of documentation. But that would be a huge mistake. The tradition of oral history—and, of course, telling ghost stories—has been around for as long as mankind can remember. So we can excuse the medium to an extent when it fails to produce facts to back up a particularly horrifying tale. With or without authentication or validation, the truth is that the story remains. And it does so to remind us that all is not logical in our world. Not everything can be easily explained.

One odd turn along the road of life and we can suddenly be faced with the things we were always told were legend. Chances are, if you are reading this book, you probably know a person or two whom this has happened to. Or maybe it was you.

The truth is that sometimes things do, indeed, go bump in the night, and sometimes those things aren't necessarily supernatural. Tales such as the ones listed in this book can also remind us of the ugly elements of humankind—the horrors of war, love stories gone awry, and the malicious things that people can do. The world can be a terrifying place, and these incidents are the foundation for a lot of terrifying stories.

There is also a more practical reason for many supernatural occurrences to lack supporting facts. Oftentimes when people encounter the mysterious there is a need for the incident to make sense to the observer. It's not enough to simply accept the situation—that there's a spirit appearing on the bridge in the middle of the night for instance or that the sounds of a car crash can clearly be heard with no accident in sight or that mysterious handprints are appearing on the windows of a parked car. The observer wants everything to have a reason, so he/she makes up a story to account for the situation.

Because of this, very real supernatural events are happening all over the country, but the particulars surrounding the incidents are completely false. This is human nature; there is always a need to explain the unknown. For me, the challenge of writing a book about bridges and the supernatural involves the obvious—the familiarity and similarity of the stories.

Why does the story of a crybaby bridge sound so familiar to you and me? There's an easy answer. There's a crybaby bridge in almost every state in the country! It's a common location and they invariably have the same name. So, rather than write a book like my previous tome, *The Ghost Hunter's Field Guide* (which lists more than a thousand haunted places state-by-state), I decided to document the best bridges and tales in the country and organize them into recognizable categories.

As a note for would-be explorers, the bridges listed in this book are almost always public locations (and are noted when they are not), but care and caution should always be exercised when trekking to these spots. Especially if it's a bridge located in the middle of nowhere or down a road that is no longer serviceable. I am, of course, talking about very real dangers here—not the supernatural. Some bridges are decommissioned because they simply are not safe anymore, and never forget that a bridge is almost always made to cross over something and what's underneath is probably not so safe! And then there are trains and traffic ... Yes, yes, you get it.

So always let people know when you venture into the wilds, always do the safe thing, and always get permission if you decide to visit any private locations listed here. And remember, while the stories chronicled in this book can sometimes be debated concerning the validity of the details—or perhaps dismissed by certain intellectuals as being rumor or urban legend—a couple things are quite certain:

The bridges are quite real.

And somewhere a small group of people is gathered together telling stories about that bridge right now ...

## Chapter One
# HANGINGS AND LYNCHINGS

Bridges are an unusual location for formal hangings to take place (though this has certainly happened on occasion, such as during the American Civil War), so you can imagine that most of the stories in this chapter involve some sort of wrongdoing. During the days of the Wild West, law enforcement officials were few and far between—and many were nothing more than paid henchmen who worked for local land barons. So it's no surprise that vigilantes and angry mobs often dealt out the punishment for crimes committed in those days. But these aren't the only individuals who have been hung on bridges. Unfortunately, innocent people have also met their demise at the end of a dangling rope for various reasons—usually quite nefarious reasons. Because of this, many of these hanging bridges are now considered haunted.

## Oakachoy Covered Bridge—Coosa County, Alabama

This awesome bridge is also known locally as the Thomas Covered Bridge. It stands between the towns of Nixburg and Alexander City, just off State Route 259. Dating back to 1916, this bridge was a listed historical site until vandals burned it down in June 2001. It was the last covered bridge of its kind in Coosa County and was known for many miles around for its haunting—a haunting that is said to still exist at the site of the old bridge.

Though the bridge was built long after the abolishment of slavery, this area of Alabama was still rife with racial tensions when it was constructed. So it goes that a former slave from the area was lynched at this site (though at least one report places the hanging nearby, with the ghost simply haunting the bridge that's in the vicinity).

Haunted activity at the location prior to the fire usually involved automobiles parked on the bridge (door handles would be shaken, the engine would die, etc.). People thought this was an attempt by the specter to get visitors to leave. Now that the bridge is gone, activity has shifted to sightings of an apparition. The specter is thought to be the man who was hung, and it sometimes appears as a normal person and sometimes as a black, shadowy shape walking through the woods.

## Old Dora Train Trestle—Dora, Alabama

The city of Dora was formed in the late 1800s when the rail lines from Kansas City, Memphis, and Birmingham converged in the area. The city sprung up around the veins of train tracks that cobwebbed the area, and most people who lived in the city were involved with the railroad in some capacity. As can be expected, many accidents and deaths have occurred through the years here involving locomotives, but it wouldn't be any of these tragic incidents that would bring about the local haunting.

According to legend, the ghost that haunts the area surrounding the old train trestle in town is the product of a wrongful hanging. After a horse was claimed to have been stolen by a local

African-American man, an angry mob descended upon the unfortunate individual and strung him up on said trestle. As an added insult, it is said that the "stolen" horse was found shortly after the horrible incident.

These days, folks in the town of Dora often see the silhouette of the poor, dead man hanging in the wind. And if you listen close, the sounds of his death moans can be heard, though some believe the moans to be those of his loved ones who watched him die.

## Alamuchee-Bellamy Covered Bridge —Livingston, Alabama

Perhaps the most interesting fact about this bridge is that it originally stood in a completely different location. Though it's now on a pond in the middle of the University of West Alabama's campus, it was originally built in 1861 as a means for Confederate general Nathan Bedford Forrest to cross into the state of Mississippi. It was while the bridge was spanning the Sucarnoochee River that one of its most infamous occurrences happened.

It was during 1886 that outlaw sheriff Stephen S. Renfroe was hung by an angry mob. Renfroe was known throughout the area for numerous crimes, multiple prison escapes, and a close association with the Ku Klux Klan. With all this in mind, the town had had enough of him. He was marched to the river and hung. His body was removed from the location and is now buried in an unmarked, unknown grave. Perhaps this is the motive for him to return from the dead…

Since then, despite the bridge being relocated to a new spot, people claim to see the spirit of old Renfroe on this bridge. Paranormal activity is said to include the moans of the dead and the odd sighting of the sheriff himself. Interestingly, people have also reported seeing unusual things at the bridge's original location.

## Choctawhatchee Bridge—Newton, Alabama

Also known as the ghost of Sketoe's Hole, the haunting that involves this bridge is well known throughout the southern United States. William Sketoe was a Methodist minister who was hung on December 3, 1864. With the American Civil War in full swing, Sketoe came up on the bad side of the local home guard in Newton and was accused of aiding the enemy (most likely Union soldiers/refugees who were taking shelter in the area). It was because of this that Sketoe was hung beside the Choctawhatchee Bridge. But that's not where the story ends…

Locals say that Sketoe was so big that when the mob attempted to hang him, his weight dragged him to the ground. Because of this, the men quickly began to dig under his feet until he eventually strangled over a massive hole. Since that day, it's reported that the hole remains at the site despite being filled in over the years by various people who have visited this location—and it was even filled by construction workers when a newer bridge replaced the old one. If you visit this location and get bored waiting for the spirit of Sketoe, be sure to check out the plaque nearby and read about the tale in person.

## Euharlee Covered Bridge—Bartow County, Georgia

Dating back to 1886, this bridge was built by Washington W. King (son of Horace King, another famous bridge builder and freed former slave) and Johnathan H. Burke. It operated until recently and is now a minipark with picnic spots, a historical marker, and a small museum. It's owned by the county and closed to the public at night, so make sure to get permission if you plan to visit after dark.

As for the ghost, local legend says a young Native American girl was abducted shortly after the bridge's construction and was taken there to be beaten and hung. Witnesses of the haunting say you can hear the sounds of the rope creaking under her weight and the girl's soft cries if you venture across the bridge at the right time. Paranormal groups have investigated this site rather extensively with mixed results. Some say the creaking is a natural sound made by the wooden bridge. Some say they have not only heard the young girl's spirit, but they have seen the apparition of her hanging in the rafters.

Either way, there are no records of the dead girl listed in any of the local newspapers. The only odd death associated with this area involves a former bridge over Euharlee Creek that was washed away in a flood (a local man and his mule were drowned). Now, the ghost of a mule would, indeed, be something to see.

## River Road Bridge—Caldwell, Idaho

This old bridge over the Boise River is known far and wide—at least in Idaho—as a sort of paranormal pilgrimage. Since it is one of the most accessible haunted sites in the state, most of the ghost-hunting groups in the area have posted articles about the site or have performed investigations here. So what's the draw to this spot?

Locals claim that a woman committed suicide on the bridge, hanging herself from one of the upper beams. Now people say you can see the spirit of the woman. Sometimes she appears as a full apparition, but most often she is seen as a shadowy mass along the side of the structure.

In addition to sightings of the unfortunate lady, there also seems to be a bizarre mystery concerning a spot below the bridge. There is a small island that has a light that appears each night for no explainable reason. There is no power of any kind leading out to the spot and an examination of the area will reveal that nobody is present there. Yet the light still appears.

And if that isn't odd enough for you, also consider the strange story of the invisible splash. Visitors to the bridge claim that if something is thrown into the water below you will hear the impact but see no visible evidence of the splash.

## Zingg Road Bridge—Millstadt, Illinois

The entire stretch of this road located between the towns of Millstadt and Dupo is said to be riddled with haunted spots. Phantom vehicles have been seen driving and then will disappear right before the eyes of surprised motorists. Mysterious black dogs with glowing eyes have been spotted standing in the road and also seem to evaporate at a moment's notice. And then there's the old hanging bridge. Those who have had experiences on the bridge say you can see the spectral corpses hanging from a beam when your headlights hit them, but when you get close to the bridge … wait for it … they disappear!

Altar Rock is a location close to the intersection of Zingg Road and Saeger Road. This patch of stones near Hickman Creek is said to be the last remnants of the spot where the Saxtown Witch did her bidding. Legend says if you visit this spot at night, you will hear a scary chanting and odd moans/cries coming from the now cursed creek. And if you're lucky (or unlucky, depending on your viewpoint), you might even see the burned, black visage of the old witch herself.

## Sugar Creek Bridge—New Holland, Illinois

Not much is known about this small bridge over Sugar Creek—other than locals have been calling it "the haunted bridge" for decades. Located close to Pool Hill Cemetery, a spot that has plenty of ghost stories of its own (ghost lights and bizarre voices have been heard there sporadically over the years), this span was, reputedly, a popular spot for hangings back in the day. Because of this, witnesses say they have seen apparitions, heard moans and the rattling of chains, and have felt sudden blasts of frigid air here (in August no less).

If you decide to check this bridge out, you may want to get permission to stroll through the cemetery, too. Apparently, an old tree that once was there served as a sort of portal for the other world. If you stand where the tree was, you will supposedly experience the lynching of a person by hearing load moans, a person begging for his/her life, etc. Of course there is no record of any hangings or lynchings from this area, but according to the tale, these were done very quietly as a means to get rid of unwanted people who lived there.

## Cataract Covered Bridge—Owen County, Illinois

At one time, this covered bridge was one of the most-photographed spans in all of the United States. Located within the Lieber State Recreation Area, it was built in 1876 by the Smith Bridge Company from Toledo, Ohio. It was raised over Mill Creek to accommodate increasing traffic. Today, however, the road has bypassed the bridge, and it is now a tourist attraction, along with nearby Cataract Falls. Pedestrian traffic is still allowed to cross, so it makes for a nice walk during your visit.

As for the ghost, locals say the spirit is a man who lost everything during the Great Depression. As many did during that terrible time, he chose to take his own life. He hung himself from the covered bridge. Now people claim to see the ghostly visage of his body hanging in the wind and to hear the sobs and cries that were probably his last moments in this world. Most of the reports of this ghost (at least that I could find) place the spirit appearing close to sunset. So if you make a trip to watch the sky turn dark in this magical area (the falls may be perfect for this), you may want to swing by this gorgeous bridge to get a peek of the poor gentleman who now walks there. Well, hangs there…

## Cannonball Bridge—Vincennes, Indiana

This span connects Vincennes, Indiana, to St. Francisville on the Illinois side of the Wabash River. Being a former railroad crossing, this structure was transformed into a toll bridge to allow one-way traffic over the river. And people say it is quite the trip. The bridge is rickety, there are gaps in the planks, and (apparently) if you look into the waters below you may see a dismembered head floating by.

The story of Purple Head Bridge, as locals call this site, is well known throughout both states along the Wabash. It's reported that a young man once hung himself from the bridge, but the rope managed to decapitate him. Local authorities found the body of the deceased, but the head was never recovered. Now there's a floating ghost head!

If the prospect of seeing the spirit of a head as you cross an already terrifyingly constructed bridge isn't cool enough for you, consider that others claim an even more sinister past exists here… The headless man was, reputedly, not the only one to be hung on this bridge. During the 1800s, this old train trestle was a popular spot to get rid of undesirables, so many say there have been dozens hung at this spot. At least this is the explanation that people give when they hear moaning, disembodied voices, and screams while driving across the river.

## Bannwell Bridge—Webster County, Iowa

If you visit this particular haunted spot, you may notice that the bridge is rather new. Well, in fact it is. It was built to replace an older structure that was located at this site on Fairbanks Avenue, just outside the town of Barnum. Locals say the ghost story still lives, however. And what a story it is…

Legend says a distraught woman (most believe she had been jilted by her husband and that she found him with another lady) took her three children to the bridge and murdered them by hanging. You may believe that the spirits of those poor kids now haunt the area, but you would be wrong. Witnesses of the spectral activity say the ghostly head of the woman can be seen floating along. And, if the whim catches her, she will attempt to chase your vehicle. Can you imagine a dismembered head speeding after you?

In addition to patrolling the bridge, some say the head of the lady is often spotted chugging down the neighboring railroad tracks. With such a fantastic tale attached to it, it's no wonder that people refer to this location as Terror Bridge.

## Giblin Bridge—Mount Pleasant, Iowa

The haunting of this bridge became a big deal when famed writer Brad Steiger documented it in his book *Real Ghosts, Restless Spirits, and Haunted Places*. Since publication, paranormal investigators have flocked to this spot to see the ghost of the hanged woman. The first report of this spirit came when two truck drivers spotted what looked like a young lady hanging from one of the support girders. As they drove closer, the dead woman simply disappeared. Since that day, dozens of people have claimed to have seen the same sight.

Steiger himself investigated the bridge, along with psychic Irene Hughes, and came away with more info concerning the woman's demise. Of course, the info did come from a psychic, so a grain of salt might be needed…According to Hughes, the woman's name was Helen, she committed suicide because she was ashamed of an affair with a local doctor, and she did it sometime around 1950. During this exchange with the spirit, local press was on hand— and at least one person at the investigation, other than Steiger and Hughes, claimed to see a vague, glowing figure on the bridge.

As mentioned before, this is an extremely popular place to visit for paranormal enthusiasts, so don't be surprised if there's a small crowd there when you visit. Especially if it's a full moon—it's said this is the time she is most likely to appear.

## Jericho Covered Bridge—Jerusalem, Maryland

Constructed in 1865 at the tail end of the American Civil War, this gorgeous covered bridge once had a twin just down the way called Jerusalem Bridge. Unfortunately, the latter would meet its demise in 1928. Spanning Little Gunpowder Falls, Jericho underwent ren-ovations in 1937 and 1982 to keep the historic landmark safe for those crossing it—and it's slated for another massive upkeep soon.

The structure was erected at the end of the Civil War and its foremost ghost story is loosely associated with that time. Accord-ing to legend, Southern loyalists who were disappointed with the outcome of the war would use this bridge to hang former slaves. No other details of these acts are known, but many have claimed to see the ghostly image of bodies hanging from the interior rafters of the bridge.

A second tale that circulates about this spot involves the spirit of a woman who is, seemingly, carrying a basket of flowers and the ghost of a small girl who appears to have been burned. The woman is described as wearing clothes from the 1800s and she seems to ignore people who see her. The young girl, however, is said to approach people and seems to be pleading for help. Other activity on the bridge includes disembodied voices, cold spots, and the ever-pervading feeling of being watched.

## White's Bridge—Smyrna, Michigan

Also known as Keene Township, this small town was devastated when an arsonist burned down its historic bridge in 2013. The town is currently in the process of replacing the bridge, so it remains to be seen if the paranormal happenings of this location will carry over to the new span. As for the destroyed bridge, it was built in 1869 and was named for local pioneer Levi T. White and his family.

It wasn't long after the bridge appeared that people began whispering stories concerning a witch in the township. The story goes that the woman was beguiling and working her ways with the villagers until they'd had enough of her. An angry mob descended upon her, dragged her to the bridge, and then hung her there.

In the years leading up to the burning of the landmark, White's Bridge became a popular spot to look for her ghost. Many claimed to have seen or heard her there. The appearance of her swinging from the rafters is the most popular detail of the sightings—though the feelings of being watched and being nauseated are right behind it. It will be interesting to see when the new bridge is raised and opened if the witch is still around. Ghosts can be pretty persistent, and there are plenty of bridges listed in this book that are the second, third, or even more to exist at the spot they are today.

## Stuckey's Bridge—Meridian, Mississippi

Perched like a rusted overlord above the Chunky River, this historic landmark is one of the most well-known haunted attractions in the state of Mississippi. Closed off to traffic (and justly so—it's as dilapidated as it is covered in graffiti), I do not advise anyone to attempt crossing or even walking on this structure. You can, however, check it out safely from the banks of the water below if there aren't already people there partying it up.

Legend states that Stuckey was a member of the infamous Dalton Gang and that he was responsible for multiple murders at a nearby inn. He would take the corpses and dump them off this bridge. So it's poetic justice that when the local law enforcement officials caught up to Stuckey, they dragged him to the bridge and hung him for his crimes. Sightings of Stuckey at this spot have been occurring for many years; sometimes he's seen wandering with a lantern in hand, at other times his corpse is seen swinging from the bridge above. In addition to this, witnesses have heard the massive splashes of corpses hitting the water, heard eerie voices, seen black shapes moving in the darkness, and witnessed glowing balls of light bobbing along (supposed to be the aforementioned lantern).

If you decide to go to Stuckey's Bridge, you might want to check in with the sheriff's office. It is generally closed to the public, but it is a popular spot, so you may save yourself some hassle if you get permission to visit beforehand.

## Road C Bridge—Spring Ranch, Nebraska

The bridge that stands at this spot today is most likely not the original span over the Little Blue River, so it is not the site of the actual hangings that occurred in 1885. But that hasn't stopped the horrible act from replaying on occasion with the ghosts of the deceased.

Two people, Elizabeth Taylor and Tom Jones (no relation to the famous celebrities of the same names), were lynched by an angry mob at this spot after Taylor's son murdered a local rancher. Taylor and the rancher had an ongoing dispute involving land (she accused him of stealing timber), so when she saw him one day on her property she sent her boy out to shoot him. When the townsfolk got wind of the incident, some angry meetings were held and eventually a group of men stormed the Taylor house, taking her and her brother Tom. The two of them were carried down to the river and hung from the bridge. The lynchmen were later tried for the murders of the two people, but they ended up being acquitted. Taylor is the only recorded female in Nebraska history to have ever been lynched in the state.

As for the ghosts of the two victims, well, they are said to hang out on the bridge. People have heard strange voices, seen odd mists floating about erratically, and have even seen two pale figures swinging in the wind.

## Pisgah Covered Bridge
## —Randolph County, North Carolina

Located just southeast of the town of Pisgah, this historic bridge was constructed in 1911 at the whopping cost of $40. Now closed to vehicular travel, this tourist attraction is open to the public during daylight hours—which of course makes it hard to do some ghost hunting at night. But if you could cross it during the hours of darkness, you might find yourself looking at a pretty terrifying apparition...

It's said that the bridge was the site of a hanging in the 1920s, and on certain nights the apparition of a man can be seen swinging from the rafters. While you can't cross the bridge at night, you may be able to check it out from afar; there's a nearby hiking trail that's quite popular.

You may notice when you visit this spot that there's quite a lot of graffiti. This is unfortunate. This is one of only two covered bridges left in the state of North Carolina (the other being the Bunker Hill Covered Bridge—also rumored to, perhaps, be haunted by a hanged man), so don't be one of the irreverent who have defaced the history here. The spirit on the bridge may not like that.

## Walhalla Road Bridge—Columbus, Ohio

Take an isolated, narrow road and toss in a spooky bridge and you have all the makings of a great story. Legends about Walhalla Road have been circulating Ohio for decades—and tracking down all the variations of the tale is quite the chore. The basic story is that a man became enraged one evening and ended up killing his wife. He attempted to hide the crime, but eventually it all caught up to him and cost him his own life. Here is where are the variations kick in …

In the most well-known version, the man realizes he is going to go to jail for the crime, so he goes to the bridge and hangs himself. Another version actually has the man going to jail and being executed there; then the man's ghost is seen right after this inside the attic of his home (a mysterious place known as Mooney's Mansion that doesn't actually exist). Finally, a third incarnation of the tale adds in the detail of the man killing his dog, which is now seen as a ghostly apparition roaming the area, as well as his wife.

As for the bridge, well, the man supposedly hung himself there in one version of tale. People claim to see his apparition dangling over passing cars.

## Stonelick Covered Bridge—Milford, Ohio

Currently in the middle of a complete restoration, this historic span is the last covered bridge in Clermont County, Ohio. Also known as the Perintown Bridge, it dates back to 1878—and some say the ghost dates back to the same year.

Urban legend states that right after the bridge was built a man was lynched there. Now the bridge carries the curse of the dead man. Well, sort of. The ghost doesn't actually appear on the bridge. You, however, have to be on it to see the ghost. The way this works is that you are supposed to drive onto the bridge, stop beside a small window that's there (there's only one on it), and then flash your lights three times. Your car will then die and you will notice, if you look through the window, what looks like a man hanging from a tree in the distance. When the apparition of the man fades away, your car will then be able to be started again.

While this whole routine may sound a bit odd, realize that this haunted spot is just a small portion of a much bigger area known as Peaceful Valley. Imagine a whole chunk of a county that's chock-full of scary stories, weird tales, and odd happenings. That's Peaceful Valley. Sound like a fun trip?

## Gibbs Road Bridge—Sylvania, Ohio

This tiny concrete span would be completely missed if it wasn't for the No Loitering sign, the graffiti paintings of penises, and Ten Mile Creek flowing underneath. Located on the outskirts of town, this spot is a hot attraction for teens in the area (much to the dismay of the local police and the neighbors who live along Gibbs Road). And why do they come? To see the ghost of course!

Legend says a young girl hung herself from the bridge, and now she loves to scare folks who loiter on it. Eyewitness accounts include the girl's apparition, a misty figure who likes to follow you or your vehicle, and scary moans emanating from thin air.

I'd dare say, though, that for every account of a ghost encounter you find online, you will find a testimonial concerning kids getting drunk, police responding to a fight, etc. So check out this spot at your own risk; if the police don't pester you for hanging around, the neighbors don't try to run you off, and a group of high school kids don't destroy the haunted vibe of the place, maybe you'll spot the spirit for yourself.

## Sachs Covered Bridge—Gettysburg, Pennsylvania

When your ghost story involves the American Civil War people tend to pay attention. Especially when you're talking about Gettysburg, one of the bloodiest battles in American history. There are dozens of haunted places in Gettysburg and it would be impossible for me to plug even a fair share of them here; instead we will concentrate on this historic bridge.

Built in 1854, this structure is also known as Sauck's/Sauches Covered Bridge and as Waterworks Covered Bridge in some parts. Prior to the great battle that took place here, legend says a trio of Confederate spies was hung from the bridge—an event that was extraordinarily common during the war. At least one of the more unfortunate of these souls now haunts the bridge. Usually a single apparition is seen swinging from the rafters, though at least one person has reported seeing three.

In addition to this, the ghostly sounds of warfare are also said to be heard here and occasionally a glimpse of a ghostly army marching across the bridge. The Union army did, indeed, cross the bridge on the way to Black Horse Tavern and the Confederate army retreated across the structure after the battle of Gettysburg, so that may explain these sights and sounds. A trip to Gettysburg is a ghost hunter's pilgrimage and should be experienced by everyone interested in the paranormal.

## Long Lane Bridge—Millersville, Pennsylvania

While there are plenty of ghost stories involving someone being hanged, there are few that sound like they came straight out of a horror movie. This is one of those horrific stories. Local legend states that in the 1940s or 1950s, a family was living in a small house close to this bridge. Even though the Depression was over, the family was struggling to make ends meet and one night the man of the house snapped. He attacked his family, dragged them all to the bridge, and hung them.

Here's where the story branches into a couple versions. Some say he then hung himself along with his family. Some say he went completely insane and disappeared. Whatever happened, there is no old house there today, but the bridge is said to be haunted. Eyewitnesses have heard cries and screams in the vicinity of the structure, seen apparitions and dark figures hanging there, and at least one person says they have photographs of the phantom family. Sounds like a spooky spot.

## Roaring Spring Bridge—Roaring Spring, Pennsylvania

Dating back to the late 1700s, the historic town of Roaring Spring has been around long enough to conjure up some great legends. Most of these occur during the period when the paper mill (built in 1866) was thriving and the town was steadily growing.

Three tales in particular are well known. The first involves a coven of witches that were known to work their deeds in the area; they would meet in the woods relatively close to the bridge and perform evil sacrifices. Eventually the folks in town shut them down. The second story is about a preacher who lived in Roaring Springs. Apparently he was also caught up in the witchcraft craze (this motif runs strong in areas where the Amish live) and was found guilty of murdering a local girl. Some say this was also some sort of sacrifice to the devil. He buried the girl in his yard near the paper mill. Then there's the bridge.

With three ghosts that are said to inhabit the bridge, it's quite the busy paranormal site. One ghost is said to appear hanging on the bridge; he was lynched there in the 1800s for reasons unknown (witchcraft maybe?). Then there are two ghosts who are said to have been a couple that were struck by a train as they walked the tracks. Their apparitions are seen together near the bridge, though they sometimes also appear as balls of light. Be sure to take time out of your ghost hunting to see the historic sights in this neat, old town, too.

## Cherokee Falls Bridge—Blacksburg, South Carolina

If an award were ever given for Best Urban Legend, then this bridge would be a definite winner. This unabashed excuse for a high school dare is known throughout the region and is now the basis for a local haunted attraction and countless folk stories. It all revolves around a character known as Booger Jim. It goes like this…

Back in 1979, a girl named Becca had had enough of Jim's marital abuse. So she talked him into joining her on the bridge for a make-out session. But when they got there, she knocked him out and then hung him from the bridge with a set of automobile jumper cables. Now the vengeful spirit of Booger Jim (monsters and spooks are referred to as *boogers* in these parts) lives under the bridge—and he wants revenge.

If you want to see this angry apparition, you need to go to the bridge at 9 p.m. (the time he was killed by Becca) and call his name three times. He will then appear. But be warned: His neck was crushed from the hanging, so he can't give you any warning growls or shouts when he shows up. At least one witness who saw Booger Jim said he appeared with big, black burn marks all over his neck. Apparently the jumper cables were attached to the car when he was hung. Go figure. While there doesn't appear to be any documentation for Becca or Jim, there are certainly plenty of accounts concerning ghostly activity at the bridge.

## Poinsett Bridge—Greenville County, South Carolina

This structure crosses Little Gap Creek and is the oldest bridge in the state of South Carolina. It dates back to 1820 and is now part of the Poinsett Bridge Heritage Preserve. There is no longer any automobile access to the bridge, but there is a walking trail through the preserve nearby.

There are several folk tales told about this particular spot. The first involves the lynching of a slave here prior to the American Civil War. His spirit is now seen on the bridge—sometimes he is simply hanging out there, sometimes he is literally hanging there. Then there's the story of a stonemason who was apparently quite unliked among those on the team building the bridge. It's said they walled him up inside the stonework, killing him. The final legend goes back a ways. This area is said to have been venerated among the Native Americans who lived in the region. Many believe that the pale, glowing apparition that's sometimes seen walking the creek is actually a former shaman or medicine man from a tribe that lived here. All the tales are quite interesting, and what better reason to get out for some fresh air and go for a nature hike?

## Drummond Bridge—Briceville, Tennessee

Sometimes the truth is more horrible than the legend. The legend is that the apparition of a man is sometimes seen on this old train trestle bridge. At times there are the sounds of moaning and gunfire, too. This may have something to do with the history surrounding this area and, specifically, this bridge.

The structure is named for Dick Drummond, a victim of the infamous Coal Creek War that happened there in the early 1890s. Coal miners lost their jobs when a controversial law was passed that allowed the coal companies to use convicted criminals for their labor force. Angry miners armed themselves and laid siege to several prisons and would attack anyone who presumed to side with the coal companies. And thus was the fate of old Dick. He was relaxing in a boarding house when a mob busted in, dragged him to the train trestle, and hung him. He was found dead the following day. Eventually, the law would die and workers would return to normal, but poor Mr. Drummond (and everyone else who was killed during the war) stayed dead. His ghost is said to be seen on the bridge named for him.

## Scarce Creek Road Bridge—Lexington, Tennessee

This bridge, along with an old, abandoned church dubbed Scarce Creek Church, is part of a local folk tale/urban legend that's well known throughout the region. It started with the church; the story goes that a woman was hung in the woods opposite the place. Some say she was hung for having an extramarital affair, some say she committed suicide after her deeds became public knowledge. Her ghost is now said to wander the woods here. That is, unless her ghost has decided to go hang out on the bridge...

For years, the same spirit was supposed to be seen on this bridge, too. Then a bold spinner of yarns gave us this urban legend: The woman on the bridge is not the person who hung herself across from the church. She was the victim of an auto accident. Stopping your car on the bridge, honking your horn three times, and then walking a circle around your car five times can summon her. When you return to your car, her ghost will appear and accost you. Whoever made up this story clearly wanted people to sit on this bridge for a long time, which is a very dangerous thing to do. I'd just skip the bridge and look for the ghost in the woods. That legend seems a bit more... authentic?

## Clear Fork River Bridge—Anson, Texas

Dubbed the Presley Bridge, this old span located on a dirt road outside Anson, Texas, used to be a hot spot for paranormal enthusiasts. Now that a new bridge has taken over the crossing—and the old bridge is off-limits to vehicular traffic—its popularity is starting to fade. But older generations still remember going out to cross the haunted bridge outside of town.

The ghost here is supposed to be a man who may, or may not, have been guilty of raping a woman named Mrs. Presley. Whether he did it or not, the sheriff and his deputies hung him for the deed there on the bridge, and now he wanders the night moaning, groaning, and longing for revenge.

If you manage to spot the bridge off the main road consider staking it out from afar. It's unclear if the bridge is safe for even pedestrian traffic, and it's very clear that the county doesn't like people messing around on the old structure.

## Bunny Man Bridge—Clifton, Virginia

Once again, we have a story that's worthy of a horror movie. Actually it's better than most of the stories in horror movies. The legend of the Bunny Man is quite well known in the Virginia/Washington, DC, area, and ghost hunters have descended upon this small overpass bridge for many years.

The legend begins with very real newspaper articles that were posted in the 1970s concerning sightings of a man dressed in a bunny costume who was terrorizing the area. He would accost people with an ax, claiming they were trespassing. Soon, a more urban legend-like story emerged concerning the Bunny Man; it states that an asylum was closed down in 1904 and while the criminally insane were being transported to a new facility, there was an accident. All the patients were recaptured except two: Marcus Wallster and Douglas J. Grifon. Wallster soon turned up dead—hung from this bridge. Grifon remained on the loose. Soon after the accident, the corpses of dead rabbits began to appear everywhere—presumably because Grifon was feeding on them.

Grifon was never found or caught, and over the years people have claimed to have found the sporadic bunny corpse there. Others say around Halloween you will, on occasion, find the body of a person hanging from the bridge, too. It's a spooky legend well worth checking out. Just make sure you stay on the road beneath the overpass. The top is still an active set of train tracks.

## Crawford Road Bridge—Yorktown, Virginia

Located on "the most haunted road in Virginia," this old stone bridge is a popular hangout for the paranormal enthusiast. Indeed, the entire stretch of Crawford Road is quite frequented by ghost hunters. It all started with a tale concerning a young woman who hung herself from the bridge. Reportedly, she was disenchanted with her life and decided to end it all. Now her apparition—appearing as a corpse—is often seen swinging from the bridge. One witness even claimed to see the entire act of the woman jumping from the bridge, jerking to a halt on the noose, and her legs violently kicking in death throes. Gruesome, right?

Locals say the bridge was a popular spot in the early 1900s for lynchings, so that may also add to the spookiness of the spot. Toss in ghost lights bobbing down the road, abandoned homes/buildings said to be inhabited with red-eyed creatures, and dark figures darting through the woods, and you have one frighteningly haunted area.

## Chapter Two

# INVISIBLE HANDS

Part of the fun involved with visiting a haunted bridge is the ritual. For a lot of the locations listed in this book, an act of some kind must be performed in order for the ghost or creature to appear. Sometimes it's as simple as parking on the bridge. Sometimes it's a complicated series of actions, such as turning off the car, reciting lines, or even offering some kind of gift to get the spirit to visit with you. Most of the bridges listed in this chapter have just such a ritual attached to them.

Since the invisible hands mentioned here are those of the dead, it would make sense that there would be something specific you would have to do in order to get these hands working for you. Interestingly, when these legends work, it's one of the few types of bridge haunts that stand a chance of leaving behind some evidence … handprints. In fact, many of the stories told here are specifically geared toward getting these handprints to appear. If you visit any of these spots be sure to take along some talcum powder; it might help with viewing the evidence left behind.

## Old Maggie's Bridge—Seaford, Delaware

This old bridge on Woodland Church Road could have been listed in several chapters of this book—but we'll go with the most common story that involves this structure. For locals, this bridge is the spot to go for some spooky thrills; it's said that if you park your car on the bridge, the spirit here will give you a friendly push. But who is the spirit? Here's where things get a bit murky...

Theory number one states that a young woman visited the site in the 1960s to dispose of an infant born with deformities. After throwing the baby off the bridge (presumably to his/her death), she then became so distraught that she killed herself there on the spot. Theory number two is a bit different. This version of the sad tale involves an auto accident that took the lives of the woman and child. Some have even offered up that the girl was pregnant at the time and there wasn't an infant in the car. Either way, the spirits of the woman and baby reportedly haunt the bridge and will appear for those who park on it. It should also be noted that the appearance of the entities is almost guaranteed if you say, "Maggie, I have your baby!"

## White Avenue Bridge—Graceville, Florida

The town of Graceville is known for two spooky stories that just so happen to be on the same road (Highway 2/White Avenue). So it's no wonder that the tales often get mixed up or confused with each other.

The first legend takes place at Highway 2 and Jones Road and involves a pair of ghost lights that are seen floating along the area. It's said this phenomena is the ghostly result of a couple lynchings that took place there when Edward Christian and Hattie Bowman were both hung after an incident that involved the shooting of a local deputy.

Then there's the story of the mysterious female spirit on the bridge... Nobody really knows who the girl is purported to be—or how she ended up spending eternity on this bridge—but you'd be hard-pressed to find someone who hasn't heard about her. Parking at this spot on White Avenue is a favorite dare for teenagers who live around here, and it's said that if you do so, you will soon notice that your car is moving all by itself. This is, of course, because the spirit is supposedly pushing the car. If you decide to visit this spot to test the story out for yourself, be sure to put your car in neutral when you park. Let's make it a little bit easier for the ghost. She is dead after all...

## Concord Covered Bridge—Smyrna, Georgia

This one-lane covered bridge has been in operation since it was constructed in 1872. It crosses Nickajack Creek and is known far and wide for a sad but interesting ghost story. Legend says a group of children drowned beneath this bridge, though no details are ever given concerning this tragedy. Locals will give you various explanations for the incident (a bus wrecking on the bridge, accidental deaths, etc.), but no facts are on record for any such occurrences. Regardless, it's said that if you drive your car onto the bridge, park, and then place candy of some kind on the hood, that candy will be taken by the spirits of the kids.

Eyewitness accounts of these events also include details such as hearing the sounds of children speaking and laughing, finding fingerprints on their vehicle, and even seeing their car move as if it's being pushed. The nice thing about legends like these is that they are easy to test—just head over to the bridge and follow the instructions to see and hear these apparitions. Unfortunately, as stated above, the bridge is only one lane, so be prepared to move your car a lot if you attempt to park it on the bridge. Apparently traffic is still quite prevalent on this stretch of road...

## Cedar Creek Bridge—Monmouth, Illinois

This haunted location could fit in a couple different chapters of this book since this particular bridge is also noted as being a famous crybaby bridge. Popular with ghost hunters far and wide, this span over Cedar Creek has a couple different stories about it.

The first story involves a young mother who, reputedly, tossed her child over the side, murdering the infant. The second story says a bus full of children were on their way to school when the bus ran off the bridge, killing many of the kids onboard. Either way, witnesses to paranormal activity on the bridge say that the spooky sounds of children crying can be heard at night. If you park on the bridge, the spirits will push you along, and, of course, they will leave handprints behind on your car.

If this isn't enough haunted activity for you, there is also a story involving an adult spirit. Locals say a man was fishing off the bridge when a car full of teenagers struck and killed him. Since that day, people have seen his lonely visage walking along the road and crossing the bridge. Sometimes he's seen standing on the structure, staring into the water below. Maybe he's looking for the ghost children.

## Matsell Bridge—Central City, Iowa

This plate-girder-style bridge was built in 1939 over the Wapsipinicon River, and although it is certainly known for the ghost story associated with it, most know it as the entrance to the Matsell Bridge

Natural Area. With shooting ranges, equestrian camping, cabins that you can rent, and wildlife second to none in the state, you can certainly find something to do while you visit this park to wait for nightfall. All these activities can also serve as a consolation prize if the ghost fails to show up for you...

According to legend, if you park your vehicle in the center of Matsell Bridge and then turn off your car (in neutral), an invisible being will push your vehicle to the other side of the structure. Some say that unnatural voices/sounds also fill the air during this event and, on occasion, a greenish glow will surround your vehicle. Like most of these kinds of hauntings, an examination of your vehicle, will reveal handprints.

Eerily enough, there's also a dark side to this story. Locals say that the spirit at this site remembers who has parked on the bridge, and if you try this more than once, the ghost will take offense and push your car across the bridge and right off the road into the river below. So give it a shot and document the activity. After all, you can't bring anyone back to show them the haunting a second time, right?

## Old Richardsville Road Bridge
## —Bowling Green, Kentucky

When Jeffrey Scott Holland and Mark Moran featured this span in the book *Weird Kentucky*, it became an instant sensation—as well as a must-see tourist attraction for the area. Numerous visitors, as well as locals (especially of the high school persuasion), have made the trek out to the old truss bridge to test the urban legend.

Dating back to 1889, this old structure is said to be the wandering place of a young woman who died after leaping or falling into the Barren River below. Apparently she is a lady of some strength. The story goes that if you park your car on the bridge, put it in neutral, and wait long enough, the ghost will push your vehicle across to the other side.

At the time I'm writing this book, the bridge is closed to traffic. However, it is supposed to open sometime in the near future, so you may be lucky enough to test the story when this book hits the shelves. If nothing happens when you venture across and park, take heart; at least you got to visit a wonderful old landmark in this area. The bridge is officially listed in the National Register of Historic Places and, who knows, you may run into a small crowd of cars waiting to try out the place for themselves, too.

## Wainwright Bridge—Jefferson City, Missouri

Here is an odd variant of the typical pushing/invisible hands story. It's said that parking your car on this bridge (a risky proposition since traffic does still flow pretty heavily across this span) and placing it in neutral will cause your vehicle to mysteriously roll along until it is off the bridge. But rather than seeing handprints of any kind on your vehicle, people say you will see bloody footprints leading from the water below to the edge of the bridge.

If you ask why this particular event occurs, locals will promptly tell you that Wainwright Bridge has had an inordinate amount of carnage and missing persons associated with it. I, of course, attempted to find stories about such things, but the search came up dry. Ultimately, the entire affair here is the stuff of urban legend, but that's not to say your car won't roll off the bridge if you park it there. Just don't get hit by any oncoming vehicles. I don't know if I'd spend much time looking for bloody footprints, though…

## Union Covered Bridge—Paris, Missouri

Dating back to 1871, this historic bridge was built over Salt River to connect Paris and Fayette. It was named after a local church (Union Church) and was added to the National Register of Historic Places in 1970. While we know quite a bit about the history of this structure, the same cannot be said of the haunting that takes place here…

Everyone knows the ghost story locally, but there's just not much to the tale. The spirit is said to be that of a young boy who drowned in the river. He is usually seen wandering the bridge and the banks below—and, on occasion, he's said to enjoy touching people who visit here. The ghost here is not the typical invisible hands type of spirit; he doesn't seem to be into pushing cars, climbing on vehicles, etc. He likes to hang out and, sometimes, give you a friendly pat. If it doesn't seem like he is going to appear for you when you visit, then you may consider just checking out the bridge itself. It is a rare sight in this part of Missouri and the history makes it worth the trip.

## Holicong Road Bridge—Buckingham, Pennsylvania

This tiny bridge over Lahaska Creek is but one attraction on a stretch of road that is known for dark legends. We should start with gravity hill where your car is said to be pushed by a pair of… well, unique… hands. The hands of a ghost? Sort of. How about the hands of a dead witch! Tales of an evil spirit that was once a witch are told about this area. Sightings of her apparition, as well as a shadowy figure also said to be an incarnation of her, happen on the bridge and on the stretch of road leading up to it.

Then there's a second, more ominous story about this road. It just happens to be true. In 1977, a young girl was murdered and dumped in the vicinity of Church Hill. But she wasn't just murdered; she was found naked and gutted like a deer. The killer was never caught, though there is a person of interest who's still under investigation. This death has been purported to be part of a ritual—either Satanic or witch driven—with the practitioners still residing in the area. These rituals are also said to be the source of many of the disembodied moans and groans heard along the road, as well as the occasional spook light that's seen.

The murder does seem a bit extreme, but it may be a stretch to call it ritualistic. It's also worth noting that stories about the evil on the road predate the murder. A bit of caution may be in order if you decide to explore these legends; this road is extremely small and narrow and lights are few and far between. There is a historic bed and breakfast nearby, so maybe that would suit your needs for a haunted visit along Holicong Road.

## Rishel Covered Bridge
## —East Chillisquaque Township, Pennsylvania

It's estimated that this antiquated structure (listed on the National Register of Historic Places) may be the oldest covered bridge in the country. It's at least the oldest in Pennsylvania. Constructed in 1830 and standing over Chillisquaque Creek, the span is only open to pedestrian traffic, which makes it quite accessible for those who want to look for ghosts here. However, it's going to make testing the summoning ritual a bit difficult...

You're supposed to place baby powder on your car and sit in the middle of the bridge for ten minutes in the dark. Once you've left the area, you will find that there are now little fingerprints all over your vehicle. These are supposed to be the handprints of little children who were murdered on the bridge in the early 1900s.

Since you can't drive on this bridge, this will have to remain in the realm of legend. However, you may be able to look and listen for other ghostly activity at this site. People have heard the disembodied voices of children playing and/or crying, seen misty apparitions, and felt intense cold spots while exploring this beautiful bridge.

## Hunsecker's Mill Covered Bridge —Lancaster, Pennsylvania

Often referred to as Mondale Bridge (because of its proximity to Mondale Road), this bridge is the spot for a popular dare with local high school students. It goes like this: If you park your car on the bridge and turn it off, the ghost of a little Amish girl will appear and crawl all over your car. Some claim that she will even leave little handprints on your vehicle.

Dating back to 1843, this bridge has been washed away multiple times by floods and was last replaced in the 1970s, but there are no records of any deaths involved with any of that. There are certainly Amish people who live in the area who most likely use the bridge, but that's about as much fact as you're going to get out of this story.

This is urban legend at its finest—and a dangerous one to boot since it's encouraging teenagers to park on a bridge at night with their car turned off. Perhaps some experimenting should be done near the bridge to see if an apparition will appear—somewhere where you won't be struck by oncoming traffic…

## Devenger Road Bridge—Greer, South Carolina

There's not much to say about this simple concrete span over Brushy Creek; it doesn't have any history to tell of, it's not ornate in any way, and it certainly isn't unique. It does, however, have an interesting ghost story/urban legend…

A woman was driving home after trick-or-treating with her kids when she realized she left something important in her trunk. So she pulled over in the vicinity of the bridge and was struck and killed by traffic as she was walking to the rear of her vehicle. Because of this, people say that if you park your car on this bridge, her ghost will push your vehicle off of it. You may have to have it stopped and in neutral in order for her to have the strength to do this, but that's the legend in a nutshell.

As always, the bigger scare here is the prospect of stopping on the bridge, especially since there's no shoulder. You would actually be stopping in the street. So this is a tale best not tested.

## Brushy Creek Bridge—Hutto, Texas

Known far and wide as Jake's Bridge, this basic concrete structure over Brushy Creek is known for a sad and interesting legend. Jake was a family man during the Depression era who went broke when the price of cotton plummeted. When things got rough, his depression deepened. When ends couldn't meet any more, Jake snapped. He killed his wife and kids, thought about what he had done, and then went to the bridge (a previous incarnation that stood at this spot in the 1930s) and hung himself.

Adventurers now journey to the bridge in Hutto to see if Jake is still around. You're supposed to park on the end of the bridge—either is fine—and put your car in neutral. After a few seconds, your car will begin to move and it will roll until it is off the bridge. Then it stops. Back in the day, when this tale was first told, the roads between Hutto and Pflugerville were all dirt, so it was easy to see the handprints in the dust on your car after Jake gave you a push. Now, with the roads all paved, you will have to use powder or dirt to test the tale. Of course, if you don't want to stop in the road (smart move), the entire area is said to be haunted by Jake. It's actually known as Jake's Hill.

## Barnes Bridge—Sunnyvale, Texas

Located along Barnes Bridge Road in the vicinity of Lake Ray Hubbard, this nondescript bridge would be passed without a glance were it not for the ghost story associated with it.

It's said that in the 1970s a woman was on her way home with her child when they hit a patch of bad weather. The car skidded, flipped, and ended up in the water near this bridge. Both were killed in the accident. Now, if you park on the bridge, turn your car off, and place your keys on the ground, a strange thing is supposed to happen—nothing. Well, nothing immediate anyway. Pick your keys up after three minutes, drive away, and then check your car. You will supposedly find small fingerprints all over your vehicle.

Of course, if you park your car on the bridge, get out, and get struck by a passing vehicle, you may be the next ghost that leaves fingerprints on cars. Don't do it. Be safe and check out some of the other haunted places in the area that don't involve traffic and parking on bridges.

## Canal Bridge—Prosser, Washington

This dinky bridge over a small canal/irrigation ditch is the site of a two-part haunting. In itself, it's not much of a tale; a young girl was seen leaping from the bridge to the water below. Presumably this is a glimpse of a past act involving her death. On its own, it's a rather boring ghost story. However, nearby is an infamous gravity hill located on North Crosby Road (you can actually Google this spot and find it marked on the map—the bridge is within sight of the hill). It's said if you park your car here, put it in neutral, and wait for a moment, your car will begin rolling uphill all by itself.

Many who test the theory put talcum powder on the trunk of their cars so they can see fingerprints left there by the spirits who are pushing them. Legend trippers say the spirits are those of several young girls who perished in an auto accident at this spot. Others say they are children who died in a school bus incident. Neither is probably true, but the hill does seem to work. Give it a try.

## Chapter Three

# SAD SUICIDES

This was, easily, the hardest chapter to write in this book. All of these locations are associated with actual, real-life events that involved the loss of human life in the worst possible way. When a soul has reached a point of extreme desperation or depression and then exits this world, a sad spirit is then created. Sometimes these forlorn souls stick around and become ghosts, like those in the stories documented here. Sometimes they move on to the next world. When visiting these locales, always keep in mind that the dead here were once very real people. So be respectful of the history and those who perished by their own hands.

## Mossdale Bridge—Lathrop, California

Extreme care must be taken if you plan to visit this haunted bridge —but this isn't because of any ghost that resides in the area. This is due to the fact that this bridge is a train trestle rather than a crossing for automobiles. And trains *do* cross here. So beware! That said, the trestle here is a common destination for ghost hunters.

The haunting of the young man who committed suicide at this location is known throughout the state. According to those who have seen the spirit on the bridge, he appears to be a male in his twenties or thirties, wearing a pair of jeans and red-checkered flannel shirt. The bridge dates back to 1928, but legend says the suicide occurred in the 1970s. Unfortunately, not much is known about the backstory of the poor deceased man.

It should be noted that this particular ghost seems to be of the residual type. Rather than interacting with onlookers, the entity ignores everything around him. As a result, this should be a relatively tame haunt for those who are brave enough (and safe enough) to visit this location over the San Joaquin River.

## Colorado Street Bridge—Pasadena, California

How many suicides does it take for a bridge to be known nationwide as a "suicide bridge"? Four? Twenty? How about more than a hundred! It's the sad but very real truth about this bridge that crosses the Arroyo Seco River. To make it even worse, this name was given to the location in the early 1930s.

Local documentation lists the first suicide at this bridge took place on November 16, 1919, a mere seven years after it was built in 1912. Deaths would spike considerably during the Great Depression and World War II, but they would never quite go away. It's estimated that by the 1940s more than a hundred people died making the 150-foot jump.

In 1993, the bridge was overhauled to become safer—and a huge barrier was constructed to deter people from jumping over the side. The wall has made a huge difference, and suicides have drastically decreased since it was erected, but the massive death toll over the decades has led to one unusually active haunted location.

Of the ghostly tales told about the bridge, perhaps the most dramatic is that of a woman who is seen in a white dress leaping from the ledge. It's said that she disappears before hitting the ground, but it would be a terrifying sight nonetheless. Other spirits spotted on the structure include a man who appears in retro clothing and wire-rimmed glasses and a woman who calls out for her baby (according to legend, she intended to kill her baby by throwing him/her over the side, then jumping herself—however, the baby lived). But that's just the tip of the haunted iceberg...

There are also ghosts seen underneath the bridge. One spirit is said to be that of a worker who died in the wet cement while the bridge was being built. Another is said to be a man who mumbles something about his death being "her fault." On top of all this, many who investigate this area often hear the odd cries of the dead, bizarre screams, and even spooky laughter. It all adds up to one of the most well-known haunted bridges in all of America.

## Comstock Covered Bridge—East Hampton, Connecticut

Named after General Comstock, a local military luminary from ages past, this covered bridge is one of only three such structures in the state of Connecticut. It was built to span the Salmon River and is now the main attraction at a small park on the verge of the Salmon River State Forest. Interestingly, nobody seems to agree as to when the bridge was actually built. Some sources date it back as far as 1791, but the general consensus says either 1840 or 1873. Either way, today it is a pedestrian-only bridge, so you need not fear traffic while exploring this landmark.

As for the ghost story—well, it's a sad tale, indeed. The legend states that a young couple used the bridge for nightly meetings. Things were getting serious until the girl abruptly decided to end the relationship. Distraught, the boy would still come to the bridge every evening, even leaving notes there, hoping she would one day return to him. Eventually, it became apparent that she was never going to return, and the boy despaired. He hung himself there on the bridge. People who have seen the lonely spirit say he will appear briefly, moaning "Why?"

## Nineveh Falls Bridge—Killingworth, Connecticut

This entire area is part of a dam and spillway for Lake Hammonasset—and there are actually two bridges that are near the falls (the highway bridge and a small pedestrian bridge). Since the legend surrounding this location involves the actual falls, you can attempt to experience the haunting from either bridge.

According to legend, a young Native American couple said good-bye at this spot. The man was going to war along with the warriors to fight a rival tribe; the woman would be waiting for his return. The battle, however, did not go so well. Most of the men were killed, and the young man was numbered among the dead. The woman did not take this well. She climbed to the top of the cliffs and leaped to her death in sorrow. Sadly, the news of the warrior's death was incorrect. When he returned to the village, he found that his love had committed suicide in his name. Distraught, he declared he would join her in death, so he scrambled to the top and made the same leap.

Some say the fall killed the warrior—others say he actually survived and went on to live a long life. For those who have had ghostly encounters at the falls, this detail is moot. It's said the sounds of the woman's wails of grief can be heard echoing throughout the area, and, on occasion, the misty figure of the sad woman is seen in the trees.

## Napoleon Bonaparte Broward Bridge
## —Jacksonville, Florida

Known locally as Dames Point Bridge, this structure was just completed in 1989. The bridge stands 175 feet over the St. Johns River. Despite its short life, this location has already had a fair share of suicides.

As for the ghost story… well, there's not a whole lot to it. Apparently people have occasionally seen the spirit of a young African-American woman walking along the span. Attempts at researching who this woman could be have turned up nothing. In recent memory, only one African-American woman has fallen from this area—and, strangely enough, she survived. Many have surmised that the entity is a product from the past that has wandered over to the site. Others say the woman was murdered nearby and thrown into the river.

Choose whichever story you like the best and make a visit to this awesome cable-stayed bridge. Just be careful of traffic; the woman who fell off this bridge (and lived) was pushed by a passing vehicle after her car sustained a flat tire and she had gotten out to change it.

## Love Ford Bridge—Jasper County, Illinois

Located outside the town of Newton, this arch/span bridge along East 1400th Avenue was built in 2004 to replace the old one that crossed the Embarras River. Besides being in an area that's known for a few haunted places, the bridge itself is said to be the wandering area of a male spirit that's seen lying facedown in the river. It's said he committed suicide from the old bridge and that his presence can be felt when you are in the spot he jumped from.

In addition, Love Ford Bridge is also said to host the ghosts that wander over from nearby Higgins Cemetery (also known as Coburn Cemetery). These specters include deceased Satanic worshippers, mysterious ghost lights that bounce along, and dark masses that seem to scoot along the ground. Eyewitness accounts of the paranormal at this bridge usually include bizarre moans, chants, and screams that seem to emanate from the distance. Most believe these are also coming from the old cemetery, but at least one person has claimed that the sounds began right after seeing the pale body floating in the waters below the bridge.

## Brooks Bridge—Martin County, Indiana

Located just outside the towns of Shoals, Lacy, and Whitfield, this bridge was constructed over the White River in 1894. It was recently renovated, however, and is quite sturdy for its age.

The ghost story concerning this site has been circulating for at least two decades and involves a young girl who committed suicide off the bridge. It's said that she was distraught—either because of losing her betrothed or general depression, depending on who you ask—and that her spirit now reenacts her last moments on the fifth night of each month. According to those who have seen the spirit, or at least tell the tale about her, she stands on the bridge for a moment and then crawls over the edge where she leaps with a scream into the waters below. But there's more to the story…

Some say that if you manage to accost the ghost before she accomplishes her deed, she will turn on you and immediately give chase. It seems that she does not like to be interrupted when it is time to make the leap. No historical records have turned up to support the story of the suicide, but people claim that the tale has been around for so long that it would be impossible to track down the specific incident. Take a look-see for yourself.

## Cumberland Falls Bridge—Corbin, Kentucky

The Cumberland Falls State Park is a wonder all to itself. With lush landscapes, plenty of outdoors activities to do, and the chance to see a magical "moonbow," it makes for an awesome getaway. Toss in a cool ghost story and, well, it's unmissable, right?

The ghost story has less to do with the actual bridge and more to do with the neighboring falls. The legend states that a couple was about to be married at the old lodge when the groom was a no-show. Apparently he was killed in an auto accident. Upon receiving word of his death, the bride climbed to the top of the falls and threw herself off. Another version of the story also exists. It states the couple was actually on their honeymoon and were simply taking photos and enjoying themselves on the bridge when she tumbled to her death.

Either way, the area of the accident is now a famous Lover's Leap in Kentucky, and sightings of this unfortunate woman are quite common. She is usually spotted wearing a white wedding dress and is almost always in the vicinity of the cliff top. It's also noted that the spirit seems to be fond of the aforementioned moonbows. What's a moonbow? It's a natural phenomenon that involves moonlight reflecting off moisture in the air to create a nighttime rainbow. Cumberland Falls is one of the few places that can reliably produce such an event, and when it happens don't be surprised if you notice a spectral spectator checking out the event with you.

## Trowbridge Road Bridge—Bloomfield, Michigan

This location seems to be riddled with questions. The biggest being, "Is it actually haunted?" Local legend trippers say yes. Word has it that depressed individuals used this span as a means to commit suicide. Though it's not a particularly high bridge, there are train tracks beneath it. So people say that those who did not die from the fall typically got hit by a train. Doesn't sound like a pleasant way to die.

I could find no news coverage concerning any suicides at this spot—but then a lot of news outlets won't print suicide deaths in the paper. So there's no way to confirm if anything of this sort has actually happened. Either way, visitors claim that they see apparitions of children on the bridge and hear screams in the area.

Before you visit this particular location, though, I should give a couple warnings. First off, there are train tracks, so be careful! Second, it seems that local authorities frown upon people hanging around here and have been known to give tickets for trespassing (even though it seems that the spot is public property). So consider yourself warned on both fronts.

## Fallasburg Bridge—Lowell, Michigan

Built in 1871 by Jared N. Bresee for the whopping sum of $1,500, this historical landmark is one of the few remaining covered bridges in Michigan open to vehicular traffic. If you visit this site in the daytime, you can check out the marker next to the structure that details the founding of Fallasburg by John and Silas Fallas (an area also known as Vergennes Township), as well as the origin of this span across the Flat River.

As for the ghost here, the male spirit is thought to be a sad soul who committed suicide at the bridge. Some say he jumped and drowned in the waters below, some say he hung himself from a truss. Either way, people have heard disembodied voices on the bridge and heard footsteps stomping across, and, on rare occasion, they have seen the pale visage of the forlorn man.

Since the bridge is open to traffic, you may want to just get close enough to do some ghost watching. You may also want to take a look around at other popular sites in the area—the bridge is part of the Fallasburg Pioneer District, a well-known tourist attraction.

## Mackinac Bridge—Mackinaw City, Michigan

When you look at the stats concerning this massive bridge, you realize what a feat of engineering it actually is. Connecting the Upper and Lower Peninsulas of Michigan, this span is an astounding 26,372 feet long. It was completed in 1957 and has since been a massive tourist attraction to the area. It was first envisioned in the 1800s shortly after the success of the Brooklyn Bridge, but it took decades to get going and eventually constructed.

Five people lost their lives during the work on the bridge and over the years there have been sporadic suicides, so it's not a big surprise that this location would be considered haunted. Ironically, the story most people tell concerns a baby that supposedly died in an automobile accident. There is no such record of this event (unlike the deaths of the workers and suicides), but the tale is told nonetheless.

Witnesses have claimed to see apparitions walking on the bridge. These are assumed to be the aforementioned folks who died here. Most often they are thought to be actual people, but when they are approached (or simply observed sometimes), they disappear. If you decide to take a trip across, allow for some time to visit the Mackinac Island State Park and Fort Mackinac. They, too, have ghost stories associated with them, and it would make for a great haunted getaway.

## Oakwood Avenue Bridge—Owosso, Michigan

Adjacent to the Kiwanis Park, this pedestrian-only bridge is one of the few Whipple truss spans left in the state. It was once for vehicular traffic, but when the city opened up a new bridge a block away on Gould Street, it was transformed into a local landmark for a leisurely stroll. It also received a handsome new blue paint job. For decades the structure was a faded salmon color (and was known throughout the area as the Pink Bridge).

Locals say this spot over the Shiawassee River is one of the best ghost-watching locations in the area. Legend states a pair of lovers decided to end their lives together by leaping from the bridge, and now they are forever doomed to roam. Dozens of people have claimed to see the spirits standing on the bridge, while others have heard voices/yells (presumably them as they fell into the water) and felt unseasonably cold blasts of air hit them as they cross. Since this is a pedestrian bridge, this may be one of the best bridges to check out for spooks.

## Washington Avenue Bridge—Minneapolis, Minnesota

Connecting the East Bank and West Bank of the University of Minnesota's campus, this bridge is a double-decker wonder over the Mississippi River. One deck is for vehicles and the local rail system, and one deck is for bicycles and pedestrian traffic.

Unfortunately, the bridge seems to have a darker use for some people, too. This seems to be one of the most popular suicide spots in the city. Over the years, several people have jumped from the bridge, including famed poet John Berryman, who was teaching at the university. Jumpers land either in the flats below or in the water.

Students at the university know about the ghosts of the bridge and, since it is a pedestrian crossing, it's a popular place to hang out and ghost watch. The spirits are said to be the product of these suicides and most say you can hear the footsteps of the specters around you while you're walking across. On occasion, people have also noted disembodied voices and, at least twice, people have seen the sad apparition of a person looking out over the river. Could the ghost be that of Berryman? Go find out for yourself!

## Mike O'Callaghan-Pat Tillman Memorial Bridge —Clark County, Nevada

This massive modern achievement in architecture opened to the public in 2010. It was the keystone item for the $240 million Hoover Dam Bypass Project. It's a gorgeous pedestrian and automotive crossing, standing a staggering nine hundred feet above the Colorado River—and it provides a perfect view of the nearby Hoover Dam (something that could only be achieved by helicopter prior to the bridge's construction).

Unfortunately, it seems that when a new bridge of this size is built with a pedestrian crossing, suicides are sure to follow. The first took place in 2012, and as of the writing of this passage the number has increased to eight deaths. Along with these saddening deaths, it also figures that one of the sad spirits would apparently be sticking around. At least that's what a handful of witnesses say. Glimpses of an apparition standing on the bridge, staring toward the dam, have been documented.

A walk across this bridge is a wonderful thing, and a great trip in itself. However, you may want to check out a couple other well-known haunted spots while you're there. The Hoover Dam itself is said to be haunted (112 deaths occurred during its construction) and the infamous Boulder Dam Hotel has its fair share of ghost stories, too. It would make a great place to make your headquarters during this awesome, ghostly getaway.

## Brooklyn Bridge—New York City, New York

Once you hear all of the tales told about the infamous Brooklyn Bridge, your first instinct will be to say the structure is cursed. It began when John Roebling hurt his foot while designing and scouting a location for the bridge—that foot would get tetanus and kill him. At least twenty-five people died during construction of the bridge, and Roebling's son, Washington, got a severe case of the bends from decompressing too quickly that put him in a wheelchair for the rest of his life. (The East River is over a hundred feet deep and people get the bends when surfacing too quickly from an extreme depth.)

Today, deaths associated with the span are all too familiar. They are the sad folks who decide to take their own lives and leap into the East River. It happens all too often—with many would-be jumpers intercepted by the police and passersby. Most of the haunted activity on this bridge is associated with these forlorn souls. People have seen shadowy figures scuttling along the bridge, heard screams and splashes when nobody is around or jumping, and felt sudden cold spots when crossing an area a person leaped from.

But at least one spirit on the old bridge is not associated with suicide. This would be the headless specter that has been witnessed a few times. Locals say this ghost is a man who died during construction of the bridge—a man who was decapitated when a cable snapped free. If that's not enough paranormal activity for you, also consider that several people have claimed to have been abducted by aliens while crossing the bridge. UFO's and ghosts add up to one spooky spot.

## Zealandia Bridge—Asheville, North Carolina

Built on Beaucatcher Mountain as part of the carriageway for the opulent Zealandia Estate, this old, stone-arch-style span is quite the tourist attraction for the haunted traveler. Dubbed "Helen's Bridge" by locals, the structure is the setting for a rather sad ghost tale.

The legend states that a woman named Helen became inconsolable after losing her young daughter in a fire. In a stupor, she walked to the bridge and hung herself. Since that sad day, random people have reported running into a haggard woman around the bridge, asking, "Have you seen my daughter?" Cars reportedly have problems with crossing the bridge, too. Ghosts are often associated with electrical disturbances and many have said their vehicle will simply die when driving across the bridge.

The ghost of Helen is so well known that famous writer Thomas Wolfe mentioned the bridge in his tome *Look Homeward, Angel*. If you're in the area around Asheville, a quick visit to this spot is a must—but be warned! Locals claim there is a dark side to the haunting there. In addition to the ghost of Helen, many say there is an evil presence that often appears as a black mass and is known to scratch and hit people.

## White Lady Bridge—Leroy, North Dakota

Located along a rural road that cuts through Tetrault Woods, this bridge crosses the Pembina River. Locals refer to the road as White Lady Lane, but it's actually called 132nd Avenue Northeast located between the towns of Walhalla and Leroy.

The legend that takes place at this bridge is an extremely well-known tale throughout North Dakota. It concerns a young girl who got "in the family way" with a local boy and was forced to marry him to save the family reputation. The baby was born, the two were wed, but the baby died of crib death. Distraught at the loss of her infant—as well as now being in a forced marriage—the girl ran to the bridge and hung herself.

Now the apparition of the girl can be seen swaying in the wind on some nights. Sightings of the ghost have occurred regularly enough to keep the story in people's mouths, and there's certainly no shortage of people who will tell you their spooky experience concerning the bridge. Even when the ghost isn't present, people say the location is extraordinarily frightening at night with an ever-pervading sense that someone is there, lurking in the darkness.

## Johnston Covered Bridge—Lancaster, Ohio

Built in 1887 by August Borneman, this historic bridge is now the centerpiece of Two Glaciers Park. When the road that crossed the bridge was bypassed in 1991, the county decided to build a park around the bridge, which allowed it to stay in its original location over Clear Creek.

As for the ghost story, it's been around for some time. Word on the street is that a young woman committed suicide at the bridge, and now her spirit likes to hang out there. An alternate version states she actually drowned. Whichever you want to go with, people have been telling stories about her apparition appearing on the structure regularly.

Interestingly, there is a second covered bridge in the park, too. It's called Hanaway Covered Bridge, and it's not far away. So if you're into visiting places with covered bridges and ghosts, this may be just the spot for you. Realize, though, that since they are in a public park that closes at dusk, your ability to stake out the bridge for a ghostly appearance may be hampered a bit.

## Jeremiah's Bridge—Anadarko, Oklahoma

At the time of this writing, this bridge is gone; it collapsed in 1994 when a large truck drove over it. There are talks, however, of replacing the bridge, so maybe when you read this passage it will be back over the Washita River. If not, it's no big deal. People say they still see the apparition of the young Native American along the river-bank where the bridge once stood.

The story goes that the boy used to fish and hang out on the bridge until, one day, he did not return home. His mother went to look for him and found him dead on the bridge. In one version, he committed suicide by hanging; in another version, he was found dead in the river. Either way, his ghost has been seen by many people on the bridge and is now still spotted wandering the area. Furthermore, the spirit of Jeremiah's mother has been seen and heard, too. Those who encounter her sad specter say she can be heard calling out for the boy and staggering about with a dazed expression on her face.

## Lehigh Canal Trestle—Lehighton, Pennsylvania

Sometimes ghost stories just don't have much to them. Without any facts to back a story up, or any history to lay down some possible ideas why a place may be haunted, all that's left to us is what we see or hear. Such is the case with the White Lady who is seen on this train trestle. Nobody knows who she is supposed to be or why she is seen at night walking along the tracks/bridge (some have suggested she committed suicide at this spot by jumping into the Lehigh River Canal), but plenty of people have seen this infamous apparition.

Normally I would give a warning concerning visiting a train trestle, but I don't really have to in this instance. The best spot for ghost
watching here is going to be the Lehigh Canal Park that is stationed
right next to the trestle and canal. It's a perfect spot to keep an eye on
the trestle. If you're planning to check it out really late (the park may
be closed), then also consider driving down North Main Lane until
you see the trestle ahead of you. This is also a great stakeout position
with the trestle ahead and above you. Happy hunting!

## Maxdale Road Bridge—Maxdale, Texas

Known as the Maxdale Cemetery Bridge because of its close proximity to Bittick Cemetery (which is also haunted), this small span has a
few tales attached to it. The first involves a ritual: If you park on the
bridge, turn off your headlights, and count to ten, you will see the apparition of a man hanging from the bridge. He's said to be a guy who
committed suicide after his girlfriend drowned beneath the bridge.
People also tell of a ghostly car that will drive across the bridge and
disappear when it gets to the other side. Lastly, there are sightings of
a second apparition that seems to be the same ghost that hangs out
at the cemetery. This spirit is thought to be a former caretaker of the
graveyard and he's been spotted in both places, wandering as if lost. If
accosted, he appears sad for a moment, then disappears.

The bridge is actually closed to vehicular traffic, so testing the
headlight scenario may be tough, but you can walk on the bridge,
so feel free to watch for the apparitions. Also consider a walk to the
cemetery; in addition to the caretaker, tales of a witch grave and her
spirit are also attributed to the site.

## Gold Brook Covered Bridge—Stowe, Vermont

This historic covered bridge is located along Covered Bridge Road over Gold Brook. It dates back to 1844 and is listed on the National Register of Historic Places. The bridge, as well as the entire town of Stowe, is about as picturesque as a place can get. Know those old paintings of quaint towns and beautiful landscapes? They must have been painted in Stowe. This would be reason enough to visit this nice spot, but when you add in the story of Emily, it becomes a pilgrimage of sorts for ghost hunters.

Dubbed "Emily's Bridge" by the paranormal community, the haunting of this bridge is quite well known. The story involves a young girl (Emily, of course) who was waiting at the bridge for her lover to meet her; the two of them were planning to run away together and elope. For whatever reason, he never showed up. Emily became distraught as the night passed without him coming to her, and, eventually, she despaired and hung herself on the bridge. Now she haunts the place—with a vengeance. It seems that she's pretty upset about the whole no-show thing; those who have encountered Emily have described numerous incidents. The spirit likes to scratch people, pound on cars that cross the bridge, and let out the occasional death scream. If that's not enough to frighten you, her apparition is said to look like something straight out of a nightmare.

## George Washington Memorial Bridge —Seattle, Washington

Known locally as the Aurora Bridge, this span has the second most suicides attributed to it in the United States. Only the Golden Gate Bridge in San Francisco has more. Since it was constructed in 1932, there have been over 230 suicides at the location with the first occurring the year it opened to traffic. Between 1995 and 2005, there were more than fifteen deaths alone. This is mostly due to the pedestrian access to the bridge and the relatively short guardrails. It's for these reasons that the state constructed a suicide barrier on the bridge that was finished in 2011 to the tune of $4.8 million.

When you have this much death in one spot, it's no wonder the place is haunted. Several ghost stories are attributed to the bridge, including a spectral man and a dog who are seen on the bridge and by the beach, a ghostly girl who has been seen walking along the span, and a little girl who many say hung herself from the side. This is one of those places that ghost hunting needs to be done with a grain of salt; many who live in close proximity of the structure have seen the horrible deaths here, so some respect is in order for those who passed away.

## Chapter Four

# CRYBABY BRIDGES

Legends concerning crybaby bridges are so well known that there's a location of this name in almost every state. There are even similar bridges with the same legends in Europe, Asia, and around the world. There's a good reason for this. Nothing is more horrific to most people than the deaths of children—especially babies. So there are a lot of hauntings that involve these young spirits.

The downside of this phenomenon is that the stories almost all sound the same. A baby either died in an accident on the bridge or was murdered at the bridge and now haunts the place. Even activity at these spots tends to be pretty much the same and almost always includes the sounds of babies crying. I tried to gather the most compelling of these stories for this chapter, but rest assured there are plenty more crybaby bridges than the ones listed here. Chances are you have one located somewhere near you right now…

## Pleasant Hill Road Bridge—Attalla, Alabama

Originally located on Pleasant Hill Road, this bridge was replaced recently with a brand-new structure. The original bridge was then moved to a park in Attalla to be part of an area attraction called the Junction. Dating back to 1882, it is the oldest surviving bridge in Etowah County—and all told, the park is actually the third location where it has stood.

With so much history—and moving around—it's not surprising that there are few details surrounding the haunting of this structure. What's known is that visitors to the bridge have often heard the sounds of a baby crying when crossing over it. And those who were brave enough to try, often found that chocolate bars would be mysteriously taken when they were placed on the bridge. While the story has few details, the tale is incredibly well known throughout the area, with the locals simply referring to the bridge as "the haunted bridge." With it now located along a walking path in the middle of a city park, it will be interesting to see if tales persist concerning the cries of an infant during the night…

## Lovelady Bridge—Camp Hill, Alabama

The tale concerning this bridge sounds like something straight out of a horror movie. Much like many of the other crybaby bridges listed here, the circumstances surrounding the death of the infant are hazy. Most believe it was a simple car accident that claimed the life of a mother and child—others say a pregnant prostitute committed suicide by jumping from the bridge during the night. Either way, it's the details surrounding the haunting that are of particular import.

Local legend says that if visitors go to the bridge during the night and say the words, "Lovelady, Lovelady, I have your baby," the spirit of a young woman will appear. It's said she appears insane with grief and that she will approach the person who summoned her. For those who may be a bit more reserved in their search for ghosts, it should be noted that many of the witnesses who did not utter the infamous phrase also reported hearing the sounds of a baby crying—and, at times, the cries of the forlorn mother.

Lovelady Bridge has been investigated a number of times over the years by various paranormal researchers. Collectively, they have captured bizarre female voices on the bridge, photographed mysterious lights, and have had an inordinate amount of batteries/devices die on them while working here. It all adds up to one creepy haunted location in Alabama.

## Kayo Road Bridge—Hartselle, Alabama

With a nickname like Crybaby Hollow Bridge, this span was tailor-made for this chapter. The short version of this location's story is: A baby (or babies) died and now if you leave a piece of candy or chocolate on the bridge, then walk away for a bit and return, you will find the treat is now missing. Presumably it is taken by the ghost that resides here.

But how did the baby die? That's where we get the many variations. Some say there was an accident and the baby was killed. Others surmise the location was used by local Native Americans as a spot to leave unwanted female infants hundreds of years ago. There are even tales of murder. But the story that seems to be the most discussed says that a wagon overturned some time in the 1800s and an infant was ejected into the creek where he/she drowned. Now, the child's spirit lingers at the bridge.

In addition to the pilfering of candy, visitors to the bridge have reported feeling their vehicle shaken as they cross the structure. Many say the cries of the infant can be heard throughout the area.

## Kali Oka Road Bridge—Saraland, Alabama

The fourth crybaby bridge in Alabama is quite an interesting one. The bridge lies on a road that is known for several related hauntings—each scary in its own way. In fact, the area is so well known that a horror movie called *Dead Birds* was shot here.

According to the ghost story, there was a family who lived in a nearby plantation home during the slavery years. The matriarch of the house was having an affair with one of the slaves until her husband found out about it—and bad things soon followed. The slave—by all reports an extraordinarily large man—was chained to a tree and killed. But it didn't end there. It turns out that the woman was pregnant. So when her baby was born, her husband forced her to walk Kali Oka Road to the old bridge. And there she was made to drown the newborn.

Today, the plantation house is completely renovated and is private property (so no trespassing), but tales of ghosts on the road and bridge continue. Those who have had experiences on the road say they see the ghost of a massive African-American man. Some have even seen him peering from the adjacent trees. As for the bridge, well, you've probably guessed what happens here. The cries of the poor, drowning infant can be heard.

## Wolf Bayou Bridge—Pulaski County, Arkansas

The original bridge that stood at this spot was constructed in 1924, and the ghost stories associated with this area date back to that version of the bridge. Today, a whole new, updated structure stands here. But the stories persist. It's the familiar tale of the crybaby bridge with a twist…

Known to locals as Mama Lou's Bridge, visitors have been having paranormal experiences here for decades. Reputedly, if you drive to the bridge and call out, "Mama Lou, Mama Lou, I've got your baby!" the pale specter of the deceased lady will appear—either on the bridge or in the adjacent field. People have also claimed to have heard the baby crying beneath the bridge, as well as heard the sounds of Mama Lou scratching the sides of their cars as they drove across.

According to at least one source, there is also a slightly darker version of the Mama Lou story. In this variation, Mama Lou was a witch that was well known in the area. When a local family slighted her, she is said to have sacrificed her own child at this spot in order to bring about vengeance. Whichever tale you choose to believe, reports from this spot are well known and investigators have managed to gather some impressive EVPs (electronic voice phenomena) on the bridge.

## Crybaby Bridge—Smyrna, Delaware

No official name for this bridge apparently exists, but it is known locally by the name of Sandtown Bridge or simply Crybaby Bridge. It's located on a dirt road just off Lee Boulevard. If you travel along for a mile or two, you will see the span crossing a small creek.

While the crybaby legend here is mostly the standard tale, there are some interesting differences to this particular location. Most say that the baby in question was actually a toddler—and one of some size apparently. Locals claim the child was thrown from the bridge and killed by his mother because of his abnormal size and multiple deformities. Now the ghost of that child is angry. The spirit is said to become agitated when people visit the bridge, and it is known to knock over trees (visitors say there are numerous fallen trees strewn about the area), push cars, and wail like a banshee for his mother.

There are a couple documented visits to this place by paranormal investigation groups, too. They have credited the bridge with a number of interesting events. Documented activity at the site includes mysterious balls of light shooting through the area, odd mumbling voices heard in the woods, and (of course) the sounds of the baby crying.

## Whitesville Road Bridge—Gainesville, Georgia

If you are cruising along Whitesville Road, you will notice a series of bridges—and you will want to check out the third bridge if you are in the mood to do some ghost hunting. According to legend, visitors to this particular location will be treated to the horrible sounds of a baby wailing in the night.

There are a couple explanations as to why this occurs—neither of them with a lot of details. The first involves the obvious: A child once drowned in the creek. Some say that this happened by design (the mother killed the child); some say it was an accident while swimming/playing in the water. Another tale states that the child in question disappeared and that he/she either drowned or went missing in the woods. In this version of the story, the wailing is a mixture of the woman grieving for her young one and the kid crying with fear.

All of these stories fall in the category of urban legend, since there are no verifiable facts to back any of this up. But the story is well known in Georgia, and if you ask around you just might get a couple new variations of the tale concerning this bridge.

## Stovall Mill Covered Bridge—White County, Georgia

Spanning Chickamauga Creek, this historic landmark is owned and operated by the White County Historical Society. It makes for a great day trip and has even been featured in the movie *I'd Climb the Highest Mountain*. The bridge itself was built in 1895 and is the smallest covered bridge in Georgia at just thirty-three feet long.

While the history of the bridge is fascinating enough, it's fair to say that a lot of the tourists visiting there go for the ghost story. The tale lacks quite a few details, but it is well known. Apparently, if you cross the bridge at night and stop halfway across, you will soon begin to hear some bizarre sounds. And since this is listed in the crybaby section of this book, you can probably guess what those sounds are. The wails of multiple babies/small kids crying are supposed to grow louder and louder as you stand here.

In addition to crying, people have also claimed to hear what sounds like an old-fashioned, horse-drawn wagon crossing the wooden bridge. Nothing visual has ever been reported at this location, so this might make for a tame initiation into the world of haunted bridges.

## Plaza Road Bridge—Emmett, Idaho

Crossing the Payette River, this bridge is in the middle of a great spot for a mini vacation. With nearby sights like the Black Canyon Reservoir and Wild Rose Park, there will be plenty to do if you decide to stick around until nightfall to experience the haunting here. According to locals (you may want to check this in advance), there is a spot you can camp in the Plaza Road Bridge Access Area that may serve as a great headquarters for you on this trip. If you like camping that is. Having a tent may also let you take part in the haunting…

Like most crybaby bridge stories, there is said to be the requisite sounds of an infant crying in the night. Along with that is said to be the strangely frightening spirit of a woman who seems to be searching for the ghostly child. People have witnessed this female apparition and heard what sounds like her body being dumped into the water (as if falling from the bridge). And if you happen to be camping below the bridge, she will apparently visit you, too—presumably looking for the baby.

Those who have been brave enough to stay overnight claim that they hear bizarre taps, sounds of footsteps/breathing, and even scratching on their tents—all along with the faint sounds of the crying in the night. Sound scary enough for you?

## Black Jack Road Bridge—Canton, Illinois

Some bridges seem to follow a certain formula for their haunting. This location in Canton, however, defies the formula by having many different types of activity associated with it. Ask ten locals what they have heard about this bridge (it's the first one that you will encounter while driving down Black Jack Road, headed from Canton), and you will get ten different answers. There are two proposed reasons for the haunting, however, that stand out. The first involves the drowning of a baby by a psychotic mother. The second theory is a bit less sinister and involves the accidental drowning of a young child.

Whichever is the case, you are supposed to park your car on this bridge and then one or more of the following will happen to you:

+ Your car will break down.
+ A ghost will touch your car and leave fingerprints/handprints behind.
+ The ghost will try to enter your vehicle.
+ Mysterious stones will suddenly be thrown at your car.

+ The spirit will chase your automobile and possibly even go home with you.

My advice would be to just visit this bridge and see what happens—with this many possibilities in play, surely something will occur, right?

## Cedar Creek Bridge—Olathe, Kansas

Like most crybaby bridges, there is a definite sense of déjà vu that comes with the stories concerning this structure. Situated in what is, essentially, a suburb of Kansas City, this small bridge over Cedar Creek is easy to find. A jaunt to this spot is no problem if you live in the area—and it's quite accessible for those who are planning a visit to check out the haunted spots in good ole KC.

If you want to see the ghost at this spot, you will have to follow the directions. You are supposed to park your car on the bridge and wait for the eerie moans and crying to begin. When it does, you will find that your car will not start. Finally, if you are lucky (or unlucky?), you may be graced with a full apparition of a mournful mom walking toward the vehicle. It's said she killed her own child at the bridge before hanging herself there and the pair of them now haunt the area. Just be sure you are safe if you plan to test this legend; parking in the middle of a bridge with active traffic is never a great idea. So be careful and keep your eyes and ears open for the spooks.

## Crybaby Bridge—Shelbyville, Kentucky

This is apparently another bridge that has no formal name, so the locals simply call it Crybaby Bridge. You may have to question a few people in Shelbyville to get directions to the place, but don't be surprised if they want to ride along with you to check it out.

The story behind this locale is quite popular in the area and many a person has made the trek to test out the legend. What legend, you say? Well, it's the usual story with a twist. It's said an infant was killed on the bridge and that he/she now haunts the spot. You are supposed to sprinkle baby powder on the top of your vehicle and then drive slowly across the bridge (or maybe even very slowly since you don't want the powder to blow off). If you're doing it correctly, you will hear the sound of a baby starting to cry; and when you reach the opposite side of the bridge, if you get out and check, there will now be small footprints in the baby powder on the top of your car.

As is the case with many of these stories, a massive grain of salt may be in order. But since nothing is particularly frightening or dangerous about this particular haunting, it might be a fun trip to check it out.

## Governor's Bridge—Bowie, Maryland

This bridge was built in the early 1900s to provide a route across the Patuxent River between Annapolis and Washington, DC. It is a popular commute between the two cities for most people—unless you approach a semitransparent woman standing in the middle of the bridge. That is exactly what one driver claimed happened when he struck the side of the bridge with his vehicle. The man informed the police officer on the scene that he had seen a girl standing in the road and that he hit the bridge while trying to avoid her. Of course, the girl was never found.

She is said to be the sad spirit of a young lady who lost her baby in the river below. Some say she killed the child (she was supposedly pregnant out of wedlock) and then killed herself. Some say she and her baby were struck by a motorist (perhaps even her husband). And some say she was attacked by the Ku Klux Klan and the two of them were killed. Regardless, the female spirit is often seen standing in the middle of the span and the sounds of her crying baby are heard.

Interestingly, this bridge has a link with another bridge that's not far away. To know what that is, check out the chapter about bridges with scary creatures associated with them. That location, like a few others in the area, is associated with a strange being that is known as the Goat Man.

## Walnut Tree Bridge—Millington, Maryland

Located along Walnut Tree Road, this particular crybaby bridge has the usual spooky sounds of a baby crying at the bridge, but you might hear another sound of a stranger sort—the sound of trees falling. Normally, this is not a particularly frightening noise, but the story of this haunting includes a rather strong ghostly baby.

Legend says a young mother once gave birth to a massive but deformed baby. She was so distraught that she took the infant to the bridge and tossed him over. Now the spirit of that baby roams the area causing mischief. He/she likes to knock over trees when people come around, make frightening cries and yells, and generally terrorize anyone who is on the bridge.

Like most bridges, you should probably avoid parking in the middle of the span—or doing anything else that would inherently be dangerous—but you can certainly park a bit down the way and check out the general area on foot. The creek below the bridge is thought to be the stomping grounds for the destructive spirit, so tread there with care.

## Lottsford Road Bridge—Mitchellville, Maryland

The details concerning the crybaby aspect of this bridge are the least interesting things known about this location. It should be mentioned up front that the current structure at this spot is the second to cross Western Branch, and that even the road has been a bit moved recently for renovations. But that hasn't stopped ghostly tales from circulating about the place.

As mentioned, this is certainly a crybaby bridge. The ghost story concerns a young couple that had an argument on the bridge that ended with the mother tossing her infant into the water below. Many people have experienced the sounds (and on occasion sights) of the baby here since the 1960s. The most bizarre account of the ghost actually details a driver hitting the ghost and seeing an impaled baby on the hood of his car. Of course, when the driver pulled over and inspected the grisly spectacle, the spirit had disappeared.

While all of this is certainly interesting, the reality of this spot is even more so. Local police dub this area along Lottsford Road as "the dumping ground," due to the fact that so many dead/murdered people have been found here over the years. During the 1940s and 1950s, a series of dead women were found at this spot—all thought to be murdered prostitutes from nearby Washington, DC. A dead taxi driver was also found in the creek sometime during the 1950s. It has been estimated that just over twenty murdered individuals have been discovered here in all. Most of these murders (if not all of them) were never solved, but the area is now much improved and it is not the desolate place it once was.

## Roop's Mill Road Bridge—Westminster, Maryland

Maryland is, seemingly, the land of crybaby bridges. This particular span, located at the junction of Roop's Mill Road and Adams Mill

Road, crosses Little Pipe Creek and has been associated with a pair of scary stories. The first involves a local slave owner who impregnated a young slave girl; when the baby was born, the horrible man took the baby to the creek and drowned him/her.

The second story is even worse. The Ku Klux Klan is reported to have used this bridge to dispose of bodies—many of them being infants. Locals say the spot was simply used back in the day to get rid of unwanted babies.

It's horrible any way you say it, and it has fueled many a person's nightmares that have encountered the ghostly remnants of these acts at the bridge. People claimed to have heard the cries of infants (as well as adults), to have seen ghostly figures walking along, and to have felt the interior of their automobiles suddenly become frigid as they cross the creek. Other than the awful details of the supposed acts, nothing seems to be particularly frightening about this spot, so maybe it would be a great introduction to the crybaby offerings of Maryland.

## Crybaby Bridge—Senath, Missouri

Since this concrete span located along County Road 602 (CR602) doesn't have an actual name, locals simply refer to it as Crybaby Bridge. For more than a decade, people have been trekking to this spot to do the bizarre ritual that's necessary to summon the spirit here.

Legend says that a toddler wandered from a nearby home and drowned close to the bridge—and when the mother noticed her child was missing, she ran and dived into the water to rescue him/her. Only she couldn't swim. So she, too, drowned. Now people drive to the bridge, walk onto the structure, and then recite the Lord's Prayer backward. Why? Because it's believed that, if you do this, the apparition of the mother carrying her dead child will appear and approach you.

Interestingly, this entire stretch of road is part of a whole network of haunted places that dot the area. First there are the Senath Lights, mysterious glowing balls of energy that wander the road. Then there's the spot where Hangman's Tree used to stand (most believe the spot is still haunted despite the missing foliage). And if that's not enough for you, just ask folks in Senath about the legends of Bone Graveyard and Monkey Man Road. It all makes for an interesting haunted trip.

## US 70 Bridge—Las Cruces, New Mexico

The haunting at this spot has less to do with the bridge and everything to do with the Rio Grande flowing beneath it. And this is a good thing since the bridge is a heavily trafficked thoroughfare.

Locals say a young woman drowned her child in the river and now the sounds of weeping can be heard along the banks of the water beneath the bridge. Sometimes the weeping is the spirit of the child; most often the weeping is that of the forlorn woman. This is all part of a much larger legend that stretches the length of the infamous river—the legend of La Llorona. This tale is known throughout the region and involves a woman who killed her children in a jealous rage after she found out her husband was cheating on her. It's said the woman would wail and wander in misery until she finally died—and now she continues to wail as a sad apparition.

Spanish settlers who populated the area most likely created the story as a cautionary tale. A song about La Llorona is well known.

## Sally's Bridge—Concord, North Carolina

This simple, unnamed span (Sally's Bridge is a nickname given by locals) over Clarke Creek is on Cox Mill Road—and, honestly, you'd never give it a second glance if it wasn't for the spooky tales associated with it.

Legend states a young mother named Sally was speeding home during a storm when she was swept off the road, either by a flash flood or a sudden gust of wind. Her car plummeted into the creek with her and her baby being thrown from the vehicle into the water. She immediately searched for the infant but he/she was gone, drowned somewhere in the creek. It's unclear how Sally herself eventually died (some say suicide, some say she wasted away in grief), but now her spirit roams the bridge still searching for her child.

According to the tale, if you park in the vicinity of the creek and bridge, you will hear the forlorn cries of a child and screams of terror from Sally. If you are particularly lucky, Sally herself may make an appearance. Witnesses say she appears disheveled outside your car, asking for help to find her baby.

## Hardison Mill Creek Bridge—Williamston, North Carolina

While your standard crybaby bridge stuff is here—the death of an infant, the sounds of crying, etc.—there are a couple twists to the tale with regards to this location. The big difference is the death of the mother happened while she was dressed in a cat costume! Or at least that's the legend.

It's said a woman was on her way home from a costume party when she wiped out on the bridge, killing her and her baby. Now you can hear crying at the bridge, but it's the woman weeping. Some locals say this actually happened at the old bridge that was located over Sweet Water Creek, and some say that the deaths on the bridge involved a double suicide. Whichever version you want to go with, quite a few folks have heard the sounds of the crying and the apparition of a wailing woman has been seen on occasion. If you have trouble finding this spot on your ghost-hunting adventures, just ask someone in Williamston if they can tell you how to get to the Screaming Bridge, as it's known in those parts.

## Newton Falls Covered Bridge—Newton Falls, Ohio

Being the second-oldest covered bridge in the state of Ohio (it was constructed in 1831), it is quite the local tourist attraction. To make the span even more appealing, it features a pedestrian walkway that's perfect for a leisurely stroll over the Mahoning River—or to stake out some ghostly activity.

Unfortunately, there's not much to the ghost story, though. It's pretty much your standard crybaby fare—a woman was hiding her pregnancy from her family and when the baby was finally born she took the newborn to the bridge and tossed him/her off. As a result, people make the trek to this spot to hear the spooky sounds of a baby crying in the night.

While the story is pretty bare-bones, there's quite a large constituency of people who have claimed to have heard these eerie sounds. So it does seem there is something happening at this bridge. Whether or not it is of a paranormal nature, or something entirely natural and mundane, I will leave up to you.

## Muskingum River Bridge—Philo, Ohio

Connecting the towns of Philo and Duncan Falls, this old span over the Muskingum River is a perfect bridge for ghost hunters. It has regularly reported activity and it features a walking/pedestrian path, so you don't have to do anything shady (like parking your car in the middle of it). Most of the eyewitness accounts of the haunting here are about disembodied voices heard during the night. The sounds of young children alternately playing and crying have been heard—and, on rare occasion, the sighting of a young apparition.

Ask locals why the bridge is haunted and you'll get a few different answers: The river was used to dispose of unwanted children in the 1800s, a baby died in an auto accident on the span (a popular crybaby ingredient), and some say a trio of children drowned here in the 1950s. If any of these are correct, it could account for the popularity of this spot for ghost watching, as well as the reputation it has. Enjoy!

## Egypt Road Bridge—Salem, Ohio

Technically this bridge is not on Egypt Road; it is located on a side road that has been closed to vehicular traffic. So getting to this spot requires a bit of hiking and exploring on your part—and you may want to let the local sheriff know you're planning to check out the spot so your car doesn't get messed with (you'll probably have to park it a distance away).

The bridge itself is no longer functioning, and it's unsure how safe it actually is (err on the side of caution), but it is certainly standing, and is certainly visited regularly. The bridge is covered in graffiti and evidence of much partying by locals is obvious. So why do thrill seekers make the trip out to it? Several stories are in order. The first is the obvious: The ghost of a dead infant and, possibly, a mother are encountered here. They reportedly drowned beneath the bridge, or at least fell and died. The sounds of crying are now heard here. But there's more to this bridge…

There is supposed to be a cult that actively uses the bridge for their get-togethers. Animal sacrifices have been found in the surrounding woods, Satanic markings are on the structure, and some say the infamous murder that occurred at the bridge in 2010 was orchestrated by them (an older woman was found strangled and burned at the bridge). Lastly, this spot was supposed to be popular for suicides in the 1970s and at least two sources say that a couple teens died here as a result of that, though I could find no documentation about this. Regardless, apparitions, disembodied voices, and a pervading sense of evil waits for those who dare the journey.

## Rogue's Hollow Bridge—Wayne County, Ohio

Today this entire area is known as the Chippewa Rogues' Hollow Nature Preserve and Historical Park. It's only open during summer months, so if you're planning a visit you may want to take that into consideration. Chock-full of folk tales, legends, and ghost stories, this area makes for an extraordinarily interesting trip. The bridge, stationed on Galehouse Road across the Silver Creek, is wrapped up in these yarns, too.

The story goes that a witch used her charms to seduce a young man who then impregnated her. When the townsfolk heard about this they decided to go after the woman and her newborn child. She fled from the mob to the bridge, and when the confrontation took an ugly turn, she cursed the townsfolk and threw the infant as a sacrifice into the creek. There's a second story, far more boring and mundane, that simply says the dead child was an unwanted baby who was killed. I'm going to go with the witch story since it's far more interesting.

As for the ghostly activity, people hear the infant, see the apparition of a woman, and feel like they are being watched while crossing the bridge. As mentioned, Rogue's Hollow is full of stories about the devil, evil spirits, and tales of a headless apparition that wanders the area. Visit at your own risk.

## Wertz's Covered Bridge—Bern Township, Pennsylvania

Since it was plugged in the book *Weird Pennsylvania*, this structure has become the most well-known crybaby bridge in the state. It dates back to 1867, crosses the Tulpehocken Creek, and is the longest single-span covered bridge in Pennsylvania.

The haunting at this bridge is pretty standard: A woman murdered her infant by tossing him/her off the side into the water below. Now passersby claim to hear the sounds of crying—and often say pervading cold spots seem to roam the bridge. This spot is a tourist attraction in the area, so you probably won't be scrutinized too much if you go and check it out, during the day that is. At night, well, lets just say there are a lot of ghost hunters who ruin great locations by littering, vandalizing, and generally making a nuisance of themselves. So keep it on the level and be respectful to the bridge and you probably won't have any trouble.

## Van Sant Covered Bridge —Solebury Township, Pennsylvania

Also known as Beaver Dam Bridge, this structure was built over Pidcock Creek in 1875 and is currently listed on the National Register of Historic Places. There are a couple stories about this bridge, one of which is a fairly standard take on the crybaby legend. The bridge, according to these tales, was used in the 1800s as a general disposal area for human beings, apparently. Unwanted infants were thrown overboard and criminals were hung from the rafters. It seems this was a deterrent method for dissuading extramarital relations and the commission of crimes in general.

Since it's rather close to the center of town, this bridge is now quite popular for ghost hunting. Several paranormal investigation groups from the area have posted articles about their ongoing search for answers at this spot. Activity includes the crying of babies, the apparitions of hanged men, and dark figures seen in the immediate region of the span. The bridge is still open to vehicular traffic, so that must be taken into account if you're planning to check it out, but otherwise it seems a great little haunted place.

## High Shoals Road Bridge—Anderson, South Carolina

For residents of South Carolina this is *the* crybaby bridge. The legend of the female spirit dressed in white that is seen on this old structure is a well-told tale throughout the state. The story states that a woman and child were on their way home when their car spun out and wrecked on the bridge, instantly killing them both. Now the spirit of the woman can be seen searching for her baby.

Witnesses have certainly seen this spirit over the years, but some are also blessed with the haunting sounds of the baby crying. When the bridge was still active (a new bridge now stands parallel to this one), people would stop their car on the bridge in the hopes that the spirit would appear and approach them. Some say she did just that, some certainly spent a bored night waiting for her.

Interestingly, now that you can cross the new span and see the old one across the way, people have started to report what looks like a phantom car, headlights and all, driving across the old bridge and disappearing about halfway across...

## Tyger River Bridge—Union, South Carolina

While this bridge looks like an ancient structure perched over the Tyger River, it actually dates back to 1962. It's been considered haunted almost since the day it was built, but not because of the crybaby legend attached to it. It's because of the proximity of another haunted place: Rose Hill Plantation. In fact, if you keep driving down Sardis Road over and past the bridge, you will end up at the plantation in less than a minute.

The bridge haunting is a story you're pretty familiar with by now: A woman, distraught over the infidelity of her husband, tossed her baby off the bridge in a fit of rage. Then, realizing what she had done in the heat of the moment, she leaped off after the child. Both died, she haunts the bridge, and the sounds of the baby are heard at night.

As for Rose Hill Plantation, well, the massive southern mansion is known far and wide for its ghosts. The home belonged to Governor William Henry Gist, the man known for seceding South Carolina from the Union prior to the American Civil War. Generations of his family lived in this home, died in this home, and were buried in the family cemetery on-site. And, of course, some of these relatives haunt the place. Give them a quick visit (it's a state park) while you're checking out this bridge.

## Hanniwal Bridge—Elkton, Tennessee

This abandoned bridge over the Elk River takes some work to get to. It's a healthy hike—and your best bet is to just get to the river and then follow it to the bridge. Once you're there you may notice that it is quite rickety. I can confirm this—very rickety. So don't attempt to actually cross it or even walk on it. With this ghost story you won't need to anyway.

The spirit at this bridge is said to be a mother who died in a carriage accident along with her infant. She is often seen walking along the river beneath the bridge, accompanied by the disembodied cries of the child. At least one witness has seen the ghost on top of the bridge, too—but this is also quite visible from the riverside. So be a safe ghost adventurer and avoid actually trying to walk on this structure. A good pair of binoculars will save you a lot of trouble.

## Mud Creek Bridge—DeKalb, Texas

Located just outside the city limits of DeKalb, this small bridge over Mud Creek is known as one of the most popular crybaby locations in all of Texas. The creek itself is even dubbed Crybaby Creek. And it's all because of the following story: A young mother was on her way home from shopping with her triplets when she encountered a wet spot on the bridge and spun out of control. She ended up in the creek bed, her car upside down. She was rushed to the hospital where she died. She did manage to ask about her children, though, which spurned a search for the kids at the creek. They weren't found, but presumed dead. Now, if you drive to the edge of the bridge and either blink your headlights three times or honk your horn three times (once for each of the triplets that were killed), an eerie blue glow will emanate from beneath the bridge and the sounds of infants crying will be heard.

## Sarah Jane Road Bridge—Port Neches, Texas

While the standards of the crybaby legend are here—ghostly infant cries—the story concerning the death of the child differs a bit from other bridges of this sort. It goes like this...

A local woman, who was a Union sympathizer during the American Civil War, was fleeing the area with her child when she encountered a contingency of Confederate soldiers. She attempted to drive her horse and carriage past the troops, but they opened fire. The carriage ran off the road and ended up in the river. She tried frantically to hold on to her child, but the rebels were still shooting at her. Both her and the baby ended up dead. Now her spirit is eternally searching for her baby, Sarah Jane.

People say the woman's spirit can be seen and heard in the area of the bridge saying "Sarah Jane, where are you, my Sarah Jane?" There are a couple variations of the tale (one version has her hiding the baby in a basket that ends up being swept away in the current and another version has her husband killing himself and the baby to spite her), but the end game is the same. A female apparition haunts the bridge, searching for her baby.

## Bear River Bridge—Bear River City, Utah

Though it was replaced with a newer bridge, this old span over Bear River is still known for the haunting here. And since this is a crybaby location, the ghost has as much to do with the river as it does with the structure, so it matters little that the span is closed to traffic (you can do your ghost hunting by the water).

The story at this site is a bit different than the typical listing in this chapter; according to the tale, the mother who drove off this particular bridge with her kids did so while possessed. She was driving along, business as usual, until she got a few blocks from the bridge. At that point she started talking strangely, her eyes rolled up in her head, and she began driving very erratically. Her kids, aware that something was awry, began crying and pleading for her to pull over and stop. Instead, she drove off the embankment beside the bridge, killing them all.

Now, ghostly lights and a child's voice is heard pleading, "Don't do it!" There is, of course, no way to actually know if this story is true—everyone supposedly died in the car, so how would we know the last moments that happened in there? This is a well-known haunted bridge, though, so I'm sure you could get even more details about this spot locally.

## Chapter Five
# PHANTOMS FROM THE PAST

Sometimes ghosts are not what they seem. Rather than being active, intelligent beings that interact with us, they do their own thing. They ignore us and go about their business as if performing an extremely familiar routine. These hauntings are usually referred to as being residual in nature and are not ghosts in the sense that we think of them. Sometimes these particularly active areas are referred to as portals into other worlds—and sometimes that other world is simply ours, only we are seeing something from the past. At other times that other world is a place that's much darker.

Many of the bridges listed here have such hauntings associated with them. There are also locations in this chapter that do have a traditional ghost story attached, but the story seems to be part of a documented event or is a historical location that makes the tale more compelling.

## London Bridge—Lake Havasu, Arizona
Completed in 1831, the London Bridge was not made to withstand automotive traffic. After several years of sinking, it was dismantled

in its original hometown of London, England, in 1967. Robert P. McCulloch purchased it for the planned community of Lake Havasu as a tourist attraction—and it has certainly been that. Today, the bridge spans the Colorado River to a small island from the town of Lake Havasu and it houses a miniature English-style shopping area (called English Village) with an authentic pub and souvenir shop.

According to legend, though, more was brought across the Atlantic Ocean than just the bridge … During the dedication of the structure, several attendees noticed a strange sight: Four people dressed in old English attire were making their way across the bridge—and those people disappeared right in front of everyone! Since that day, many others have seen the bizarre apparitions strolling along. The spirits seem completely unaware of their surroundings and simply go about their day until disappearing. Unlike many of the hauntings listed in this book, this seems a perfectly harmless one to hunt if you're in the mood for a pint of beer and, perhaps, a glimpse of the otherworld.

## Des Arc Bridge—Springfield, Arkansas

First off, a warning: This bridge is dilapidated and care must be taken when visiting this site. The structure dates back to 1874, and it functioned as passage over Cadron Creek until it was bypassed in 1991 by a newer bridge. Because of the lack of maintenance, it is now missing portions of decking, rails, etc. So be careful!

That said, the story most associated with this location dates back to a previous wooden bridge that stood here and a small group of American Civil War era soldiers who crossed it. The fate of said soldiers is uncertain, but the sight of a handful of them marching along their way has been seen here.

Locals also tell of other activity at the old bridge. Urban legend states that a young girl was murdered on the bridge and that visitors will often hear the sounds of her death screams in the night. Other paranormal witnesses have also heard disembodied voices, a phantom baby crying, and odd knocks in response to questions (one knock yes, two knocks no). It all adds up to an odd haunting on one old, spooky, and unsafe bridge.

## Golden Gate Bridge—San Francisco, California

There is only one bridge in the entire world that surpasses the Golden Gate Bridge for the most suicides ever. That bridge is the Nanjing Yangtze River Bridge. It is estimated that a person jumps to their death every two weeks from the Golden Gate. Suicides are so prevalent at this location that the newspaper no longer reports them (for fear it encourages others) and pedestrian traffic is not allowed at night. To date, there have been an estimated 1,600 deaths at this location—so there's little wonder that the place seems to be haunted.

Though there are many documented deaths at the bridge with specific names, dates, etc., the ghosts seem to remain anonymous for the most part. A major exception would be the spirit of the ghost ship *Tennessee*. In 1853, this ship ran ashore and was quickly demolished—but that hasn't stopped it from coming back for other voyages. Every so often, visitors to the bridge and Golden Gate Strait have seen the ghost ship cruising along the canal. Even passing ships have witnessed this phenomenon; the USS *Kennison* reported seeing the ghostly ship and noted that it made no signature on the radar system.

## County Road 194 Bridge—Aurora, Colorado

This particular bridge goes by a couple different names locally. Sometimes it's called the Smoky Hill Road Bridge, sometimes it's called Third Bridge. But to most who live in the area, the location is simply known as Ghost Bridge.

Local legend states that the Hungate Massacre happened at this location on June 11, 1864. This incident is named for Nathan Hungate who, along with his wife and two young daughters, were allegedly scalped and killed by Native Americans in the area. Those who have experienced the paranormal here have stated seeing an entity on horseback, hearing the sounds of war drums, and feeling a mysterious, cold fog sweep down upon them. People have also reported hearing the voices of girls—sometimes laughing, sometimes crying—at this spot, but it could have something to do with another story…

In addition to the massacre, a second tale is often whispered about a car accident that occurred on the bridge in 1997 that claimed the lives of two young girls. Whoever the ghost girls are, they are known to touch people on the bridge and to even give them a push while they are crossing the span.

## Kiowa Creek Bridge—Bennett, Colorado

Like most of the bridges listed in this chapter, the haunting at this location centers around an event that occurred at this spot—but the spirit is that of an inanimate object. In 1878, a Kansas Pacific Railroad train was headed across this bridge when an unexpected flash flood swept down the creek, taking out the locomotive. Reports vary as to how many were killed in the wreckage (some say three, but facts seem to point to two—the engineer and one crew member), but locals will tell you that there were two men on the train who bore the last name Bennett and that the community was named for them and their tragic deaths.

For the record, some also say the two men were married to sisters who bore the maiden name Bennett. In reality, the town was named for four Bennett brothers who homesteaded the area in 1862. Regardless, the accident has spawned a rather well-known residual haunting on the Kiowa Creek Bridge. It's said that many witnesses have seen the ghostly train hurtling along at this spot. Others have stated that they have only heard the sad train whistle followed by the ghastly sounds of the train derailing and wrecking.

## Cooch's Bridge—Newark, Delaware

To visit this historic site, you must first find it. Most believe the structure to be on Old Cooch's Bridge Road, but they would be incorrect! That was the site of the original bridge that existed during the American Revolution. The current bridge lies on Old Baltimore Pike and is marked by a historical plaque in the area.

This region is known for a battle that happened in 1777—and is said to be the first time Old Glory was ever flown. The British, aided by German troops, ultimately took the day, but it's an Englishman who's said to have been killed that now haunts the bridge. Records vary as to the death toll during the Battle of Cooch's Bridge (also known as the Battle of Iron Hill), but everyone does agree that both armies suffered casualties. There is, however, no record of who the headless British soldier is that's seen at this spot.

Eyewitness accounts of the apparition say the spirit appears in full military uniform, walking the area around the battlefield (to include the bridge). And he is headless. In keeping with the spooky traditions surrounding ghost stories like these, it's also said that the entity prefers to appear on foggy, moonless nights…

## Mathers Bridge—Merritt Island, Florida

Residual hauntings are quite interesting things. Sometimes the ghostly energy appears at haunted sites as horses and wagons. Sometimes it's as an entire army marching off to battle. In the case of Mathers Bridge, this energy manifests as the sound of hippies having a good time. This bridge was at the location of a famous restaurant and bar known as the Mathers Bridge Restaurant until it was all torn down in 1992.

Mathers Bridge Restaurant was a popular hangout for people who were into the outdoors, those who believed in environmental protection/conservation, and...well...people who were hippies. The place was so well known for extravagant good times that there were frequent complaints of noise from the locals, which led to its demise. Today, the eatery is long gone. The only evidence of the place is a nearby headless statue known as "The Watcher." A Pagan/Wiccan artist named Kevin Tipton, who loved the restaurant, produced the sculpture and is said to have placed it by the waters to guard the manatees.

As for the spirits at this bridge, they are presumed to be those who made merry in days past. People have claimed to have seen apparitions and heard voices throughout the area. But perhaps the biggest evidence of all that the place is haunted by hippies is the ghostly sounds of music that drift along the Banana River at night...

## John's Pass Bridge —Treasure Island/Madeira Beach, Florida

The waterfront at John's Pass is known for many things—fishing, dolphin watching, and shopping on the colorful boardwalk to name a few. But unknown to most who visit the quaint tourist spot, this area is also known for a pair of wandering ghosts. Legend says a pair of farmers came to their demise at this location when the pre-dominantly Confederate locals discovered their pro-Union views during the American Civil War. So what happened? They were promptly killed by Southern militia soldiers and buried nearby.

Though it has been more than 150 years since this happened, people still claim to see the spirits of the farmers. More often than not, they are seen simply walking along the road or on the bridge. But sometimes that's just part of the fun. Witnesses have claimed to also hear eerie moans in the area and to catch the smell of rotten flesh wafting along with the breeze. Interestingly, people have also seen the ghosts riding in a phantom boat just off the shore. Whether you see them on foot—or boating nearby—it's said the entities are friendly enough. They just do their own thing and leave the living alone.

## Oconee Cemetery Bridge—Athens, Georgia

The Oconee Cemetery dates back to 1856, and a number of famous Georgians are buried in it, including General William M. Browne (a Confederate leader during the Civil War), Dean Rusk (secretary of state for presidents John F. Kennedy and Lyndon B. Johnson), and B-52s guitarist Ricky Wilson. The plots are separated into two sides—the old cemetery and the new cemetery—and a small bridge that is said to be haunted connects the sides.

According to witnesses of the activity, if you happen along, around about dusk, there is a chance you will see a phantom horse and carriage crossing the bridge. It's a purely residual haunting, so don't expect any reaction from the spirit. In addition to this, it has also been reported that the ghost of a former chancellor, Walter Hill, has been seen wandering the cemetery from time to time. The legend goes that he was in the process of making some dramatic changes to the local university when he was crucified (metaphorically) by the public for the choices he made. As a result he now wanders the cemetery an unhappy spirit.

## Lickskillet Railroad Bridge—Austell, Georgia

Don't bother looking on a map for this bridge in central Georgia. It won't be listed. Why, you ask? Because it's part of the Six Flags amusement park. Known as one of the most haunted places of its kind in America, it comes as no surprise that the Lickskillet section of the park would have a ghost stationed along with the train trestle there.

According to witnesses of said spirits, the apparitions appear to be people dressed in American Civil War era attire (or at least clothing from the 1800s)—and they appear to be taking their sweet old time crossing the train bridge. While appearing to be completely residual in nature, there are two theories concerning the origin of this event. Some believe the ghosts are residents of the area from that era who are simply going on their way. Others say the entities are actually actors who used to perform a reenactment of the period for the park some years back. Either way, the spirits have their fair share of ghostly company there. Workers of the park claim a young girl also haunts the midway (and is usually seen asking patrons for assistance) along with the spirit of an actor called Joe, who is thought to have perished in the Crystal Pistol Music Hall.

## Seven Bridges Trail—Manoa Valley, Hawaii

What's better than a good story about a haunted bridge? How about a story with seven haunted bridges! Such is the case with this infamous trail in Manoa Valley. Interestingly, along with the seven bridges are two different types of hauntings, too!

Legend states that this area is chock-full of the spirits of ancient warriors—a type of ghost that's often dubbed a night marcher in Hawaii. Sightings of these apparitions have happened all over the islands, but they seem to be especially prevalent here.

The second type of activity here is a bit unusual. It seems that, as you hike this long trail over the seven bridges, one bridge will disappear on the return trip. Seven bridges going in, six bridges coming out. Besides the obvious reasons for only counting six bridges (human error being the biggest), many claim the illusion is the product of local Menehune. These beings are described as dwarflike creatures that live in the forests of Hawaii, and much like elves of Europe, they are quite mischievous and like to play pranks. If they are, indeed, the cause of this strange illusion, you may want to take along some bananas for your hike. They are said to be a favorite of the small folk.

## Clark Street Bridge—Chicago, Illinois

It's safe to say that bridges at this location have had a string of bad luck. In 1853, a steamer by the name of *London* struck a predecessor of this bridge, collapsing it into the Chicago River. In 1855, the bridge was a focus point for a series of riots known now as the Lager Beer Riot. And in 1915, a steamer by the name of the *Eastland* was docked nearby when it capsized and killed 835 people who were packed onboard to travel to Michigan City, Indiana.

According to newspaper accounts of the day, the *Eastland* was an old, rusty steamship due for the scrapyard when it loaded on entirely too many people to head across the lake for a Western Electric family picnic. At best guess, the ship was about five hundred passengers over capacity. The aftermath of the tragedy would shake the entire city for weeks.

Today's version of the Clark Street Bridge was finished in 1929 and is the eighth version of said structure. And, of course, it is considered haunted. Numerous witnesses in the Windy City have claimed to hear the frightening sounds of screams and cries for help while crossing the bridge. Presumably, these are the last cries of help from that horrible moment in time when the *Eastland* sank beneath the river. If you visit this famous site in Chicago, keep an eye out for the historical marker in the area.

## Old Train Bridge—DePue, Illinois

Most paranormal investigators agree that there are two kinds of hauntings—intelligent and residual. Intelligent haunts are marked by the presence of ghosts that interact with investigators and others who encounter them. Residual haunts are more like moments in history that are doomed to repeat over and over again. The events that surround this old railroad bridge seem to be residual in nature—almost a series of bizarre acts that seem to occur from time to time.

If you travel south on Grant Avenue to where the street dead ends, you will find the bridge just south of you. But a word of warning, the bridge is quite dilapidated and is not safe to actually cross. Just approach it and stay at a safe distance and you will be quite close enough to experience anything that happens during your visit. And what happens here? Well, first off, there seems to be a phantom train. People have heard the whistle, felt the tracks vibrate, and even heard the screech of brakes, without a train in sight. In addition to this, people claim to see a phantom man leaping from the bridge. When they peer beneath the bridge, the man is gone. Toss in the occasional scream, shadowy figures, and glowing lights and you have a pretty spooky bridge. But, again, do not attempt to cross the bridge. You don't want to be the next ghost people see falling at this location ...

## Williams Covered Bridge—Lawrence County, Indiana

Built in 1884, this extraordinarily long covered bridge spans the White River just down the road from the unincorporated town of Williams. It is 373 feet long and was placed on the National Register of Historic Places in 1981. In 2010, the bridge was deemed unsafe for vehicular traffic, so it was closed down, renovated, and is now open as a pedestrian bridge—and this is just fine for all of us who like to look for ghosts on bridges without worrying about traffic.

The haunting at this site is a textbook example of a residual-style affair. Witnesses basically describe a terrible accident that seemingly played out in the late 1800s. A horse and rider are seen barreling along the bridge and then it appears that the man is thrown over the side into the waters below. Sometimes this happens in full view of those present; sometimes just the sounds of the accident are heard. Either way, it doesn't appear to be a spirit that will actively engage you in any way. So, other than the terrible sounds of a man screaming for help and a horse neighing in alarm, it seems to be a rather tame place for the meek ghost hunter to visit. Of course, people do say you have to be there at midnight if you want to see this ghostly display ...

## Kate Shelley High Bridge—Boone, Iowa

The story of how seventeen-year-old Kate Shelley averted a passenger train disaster is well known in Iowa, as well as with lovers of locomotive history. When young Kate discovered a bridge had collapsed, she hurried through the night across the Des Moines River Bridge (the next bridge over) to stop a second train from hitting the wreckage, etc. So when another span was constructed—properly called the Boone Viaduct—it was promptly nicknamed the Kate Shelley High Bridge.

Today, the original version of this bridge stands side by side with a newer structure that was finished in 2009. Both bridges are railroad bridges, so you cannot walk or drive across them. However, it doesn't appear you have to in order to check out the ghost story. There are two popular tales about the bridge; the first concerns Kate herself. People claim to see her walking the tracks far above the ground, sometimes holding a lantern aloft. In reality, Kate died in 1912 of natural causes, and some say her ghost has been spotted in the town of Moingona as well. The second story about the haunted bridge concerns the sightings of phantom locomotives screaming along, as well as the spirits of train conductors, on the older version of the span. Both tales are rather tame and it doesn't seem that anyone is frightened after seeing either of these events.

## Goose River Bridge—Rockport, Maine

The town of Rockport was once known as Goose River, and it was a hot bed of guerrilla warfare during the Revolutionary War. The redcoats had plundered the town—and many others just like it— for the duration of the conflict, so it was no surprise when the patriots decided to strike back. A British ship was absconded by the colonists, full of goods that the townsfolk needed, and a man named William Richardson was instrumental in bringing the goods back to Goose River.

Today, this bridge stands as a sort of monument to Richardson … or at least to his ghost. It's said that after the end of the war, Richardson spearheaded a celebration that included everyone for a hundred miles. Including the now-angry loyalists to the British

Empire. Sometime during the bash, Richardson went wandering and encountered a group of Tories on the bridge. He offered them a drink, but they decided to kill him instead.

The span that stands today is not the original, but that hasn't stopped the jolly spirit of Richardson from still frequenting the spot. People who have seen the apparition say that he will approach your vehicle and offer you a drink. Yes, you read that correctly. His ghost is seen carrying a pitcher of ale. Stories of this bizarre visitation are so frequent that the specter is now known for miles around as the Pitcher Man.

## Eunice Williams Covered Bridge —Greenfield, Massachusetts

This bridge is named for a historic figure who suffered a horrific fate—and who is now said to haunt this spot. In 1704, French soldiers (along with Native American warriors who had teamed up with them) descended upon the settlement of Deerfield. Many were killed and the remaining villagers were marched to Canada. The incident is known as the Deerfield Massacre and a plaque now marks the event beside this bridge.

As for Eunice, well, she did not have to do the three-hundred-mile march north. When the mob attacked them, Eunice had just given birth, so she was not in the condition to flee. She was tackled at the edge of the river and killed. Interestingly, her husband (the town minister) and children survived the journey to Canada and would later return to the United States, except for a daughter who had been assimilated into the tribe that abducted them.

Today, the bridge stands as a tribute to Eunice and those who died in the assault. It currently is not open to vehicular traffic, but you can certainly visit it. And maybe you will catch a glimpse of Eunice. Locals claim that if you park at the bridge, turn off your lights, and honk your horn, she will appear. She seems to be confused, looking for her family. In addition to hanging out on the bridge, she has also been spotted downstream, meandering along the bank of the Green River.

## Old Stronach Bridge—Manistee, Michigan

Named for John and Adam Stronach, a pair of the original settlers of this area in 1841, this bridge crosses the Little Manistee River. It's a popular site for those doing float trips and boating—and for those hoping to catch a glimpse of some historic ghosts.

On October 8, 1871, the entire town of Manistee was almost lost in a horrendous fire that swept across the area (interestingly, that happens to be the same day that several other notable fires took place, including the infamous Chicago fires). The apparitions seen on the bridge are supposed to be a couple victims of this event— young victims. It's said that the ghosts are two children who loved the river and would visit it daily to play.

Thrill seekers who have experienced the paranormal here say you can hear the kids playing in the water, see mysterious splashes, and even catch a glimpse of the ghosts now and then. This seems a pretty tame haunting and might be a great side trip for you if you decide to visit the great outdoors and enjoy all the natural offerings in this area. Maybe a float-trip-style ghost adventure is in order?

## Burnt Bridge—Hattiesburg, Mississippi

Located along Davis Road (just off Burnt Bridge Road), this is the second bridge to exist at this site. The original was the location for the haunted tale(s) about to be told, but most say the ghostly activity continues on the new span. All the versions of the haunting at this site smack of urban legend—and locals hotly dispute which version of the story is true.

The first iteration states that a couple was driving home (some say from a prom) when an argument occurred. The woman, angry, decided to climb out of the car as it was moving and was decapitated in the process. Some say the car wrecked and she was killed in that manner. Either way, it's said her body was found, but her head was not. Her headless apparition is now seen on the bridge.

Another version of the yarn states the ghost is not headless but she is a woman who used to cross the bridge to visit a World War II draft dodger who was hiding nearby. Lastly, there are also those who claim the spirit was a person killed when the first bridge was burned down during a local dispute. Whoever the ghost is, folks say they see her quite often on the bridge or along the banks of Perkins Creek below.

## Katy Trail Bridge—Columbia, Missouri

Everything about the Katy Trail is quite fascinating. The National Trails System Act of 1968 allows unused portions of railroad tracks to be converted to trails. So when a stretch of the Missouri-Kansas-Texas Railroad between the towns of Sedalia and Machens was abandoned, the Missouri Department of Natural Resources purchased it and started this well-traveled trail. If you decide to bike or hike this 240-mile route, you will pass through quite a few interesting towns and cross quite a few bridges. It seems only natural that one of these bridges would have a ghost story, right?

The bridge in question is on the trail in the city of Columbia. Legend says that if you cross the bridge at night during a full moon you will see a bizarre phantom of years past; the ghost of a one-armed man is said to pace back and forth in the area. Void of any expression, he ignores passersby and goes about his business as if you are not there. Sounds like a pretty meek haunting—and it makes for a great excuse to break out the bicycle and get some exercise.

## Riverside Bridge—Ozark, Missouri

Known to locals as Green Bridge, this spot is connected to another nearby structure, the Riverside Inn. Obviously, they are not connected physically (although a bridge leading into an inn would be quite a sight)…They are both associated with a specter that I will dub Green Man.

Stories of a green apparition that sometimes appears as a ball of light first started in the inn. It's supposed that the ghost is a former owner of the establishment by the name of Howard Garrison. He died of natural causes in the inn and his apparition has been seen there ever since. Not long after these stories began emerging, though, people also began telling similar stories about the bridge located close by. Sometimes a green spirit would be seen walking the bridge; sometimes he would appear as an ordinary ghost dressed in a black suit. Most everyone believes that the sightings at both spots are the same entity—Green Man Garrison—and it does seem that the common factor of the color green is quite the coincidence if the truth is otherwise.

If you would like to make a ghost-hunting trip to Ozark, consider staying at Riverside Inn to begin your investigation. The most haunted room there, where Howard passed away, is now known as the Green Room (naturally). But you may want to make that trip soon; word on the street is that the Riverside Bridge may be demolished in the near future.

## Darr Bridge—Cherry County, Nebraska

Also known as the Niobrara River Bridge, there's not much to say about this particular structure. It's a simple concrete span on Interstate 80 (I-80) between the towns of Cozad and Lexington that most people would pass over without a second look. Unless of course that second look happened to be into the rear view mirror and a particularly strange scene was taking place.

People say that when you cross this bridge there's a chance that you will see the ghost of an old-time pioneer woman after you pass by. The legend states the woman was killed in a wagon accident at this spot along with her child. I should probably mention though that some say a very specific set of circumstances have to be in place for the spirit to appear. Apparently your best odds for a ghostly encounter are at midnight on a foggy evening, though that would seem to make it kind of hard to see anything on the bridge, much less a ghost. As an added note, most say the entire area around the bridge/ river is in a time slip (a place where people can see through time). If that's the case, then (technically) the woman isn't really an apparition at all. You're simply looking at the woman across time.

## 295 Avenue Bridge—Platte Center, Nebraska

Shell Creek is the site of this sad, residual-style haunting—and this bridge perched on the southern outskirts of Platte Center makes a great spot for staking it out. Well, the area around the bridge anyway.

Locals say that a trio of ghostly men can be seen at the creek, lanterns in hand, digging away for a few moments before they appear startled and disappear. They aren't surprised by you, or any other visitor who is watching; you are supposedly watching the last few moments of these guys' lives. Apparently they were digging at this spot when the ground collapsed, dumping the men, rocks, dirt, etc. into a hollowed-out cave below them. They were all killed in the accident and are now doomed to repeat the event over and over again.

If you manage to see this unique sight, don't be sad at the demise of the spirits or attempt to dig them out. You are just watching the horrible event play out, trapped in time, rather than seeing actual ghosts trapped in the area.

## Ledyard Bridge—Hanover, New Hampshire

Connecting the cities of Hanover, New Hampshire, and Norwich, Vermont, this bridge was originally a covered structure that dated back to 1859. Named after famed explorer John Ledyard, the new structure over the Connecticut River is actually the third incarnation and was finished in 2000. The ghost, however, dates back to the first bridge.

It's said a young boy decked out in 1800s-style attire is often seen standing either at the entrance of the crossing or on one of the pedestrian walk areas that run along both sides of the span. Like most residual-style haunts, the spirit simply stands and does his own thing, ignoring all who pass by. Sometimes a witness will add that the boy seems to be watching for something or someone on the river—and that after a moment of wistful staring will simply disappear.

With the regularity of activity and accessibility of the area, this is probably a great place for a budding ghost hunter to check out. Just be careful of the heavy traffic that crosses between the two cities—and stick to the pedestrian walkways where the ghost is said to often appear—and it should be a great trip.

## Old Mine Road Bridge—Warren County, New Jersey

The history of this road is quite astounding. Dating back to the 1600s, it is one of the longest and continuously operating roads in America. Some believe the road is, technically, even older than that; apparently the road was built on an old Paleo-Indian trail that dates back as far as 10,000 BC. The story about the bridge over Flat Brook concerns much more recent history.

Legend says a motorist struck and killed a pair of kids who were playing on the bridge, and now the spirits of those two children can be seen and heard here. This is a sad tale in itself, but when it's coupled with the stories concerning the nearby Shades of Death Road, well...

Featured many times in the paranormal press, Shades of Death is a notoriously haunted, and just plain weird, road. Stories about the place includes three documented murders (they occurred in the 1920s and 1930s); mist creatures that populate Ghost Lake; apparitions that hang out in an old, dilapidated barn; and shape-shifting Native American spirits! So, while the haunting of this bridge may seem a bit mild, it's all part of a bigger volume of folklore that surrounds this area. Visit the nearby town of Hardwick and you may discover even more tales about the area and its odd mixture of history and legend.

## Bostian Train Bridge—Statesboro, North Carolina

This listing tells two tales—one of legend mixed with fact and one that's cautionary and very real. The first story deals with a horrific train accident that occurred on August 27, 1891. A train was traveling over this bridge when it derailed and sent multiple cars careening below. More than twenty people were killed in the accident, and it's said that on the anniversary of this event each year you can hear (and sometimes see) the reenactment of this event on this massive stone trestle.

Now, the second story… A group of ghost hunters decided to investigate this story and went out on the trestle to see if they could document any activity at the site. It was the anniversary of the accident, and, against better judgment (and advice that's been dished out in this book quite often), the group was actually walking on the train tracks. Guess what happens next… A train came that sent the group running for their lives. All but two made it to the end of the bridge. One fell to the area below the span and lived, and one was crushed by the oncoming train.

The last thing a ghost hunter ever wants to happen during an investigation is to become a ghost. So heed my advice: Check out the haunted bridges, but do not venture onto bridges with traffic or trains. Stake out the structure from afar and stay safe.

## Garfield Park Bridge—Garfield Heights, Ohio

Sometimes it's refreshing to hear a nice story about a haunted bridge. Such is the case with this location. There were no murders or suicides at this spot. No auto accidents or babies thrown over the side. Nothing out of the ordinary can actually be said about this particular area—except, of course, that there is a ghost that likes to hang out here.

For years, witnesses have claimed to see the apparition of an old man fishing off the bridge. When he's visible, he basically ignores everyone and has a good old time doing his favorite pastime. When he's not visible, people say he likes to whisper in the ears of those who are walking across his fishing spot. Some have said you can tell when he's around because of a massive, startling cold spot that lies along the edge of the bridge. Nobody knows who the man is, though most will tell you that he is one of the many buried nearby in Cavalry Cemetery.

If you take a walk through this park to catch a glimpse of this delightful spirit, you might also want to take a lap through the cemetery. You just may run across a tombstone that has a fish on it, or some other hint that will solve the mystery of the fishing ghost.

## Everett Covered Bridge—Peninsula, Ohio

Located within the Cuyahoga Valley National Park, this particular covered bridge is about as picturesque as one can be. Spanning Furnace Run (a creek with an unusual name), it stands in all its red glory against a beautiful landscape. It's a great spot to include in your trip to the park, to take a nice photo, and to do some ghost watching.

The exact date of the structure's construction is in doubt—most likely in the 1860s or 1870s—and is said to have been in response to a tragedy that is now memorialized on a plaque beside the bridge. It tells the story of a farmer named John Gilson and his wife, who in 1877 were trying to cross the creek during a winter ice storm. The two of them, along with their horse-drawn wagon, were drawn beneath the ice into the creek. She managed to escape, but he did not. His body was found four days later.

Today, the spirit of Mr. Gilson still crosses the creek. Only now he actually uses the bridge. If you're around for the ghostly event you will, supposedly, hear the sound of a horse and wagon clomping across the span. In addition to this, a misty figure has also been spotted at the bridge, but some argue that entity is actually a product of the nearby cemetery where other sightings like this have been documented.

## Karla's Bridge—Catoosa, Oklahoma

This small bridge over a tributary of Bird Creek can be found on 161st East Avenue on the outskirts of Rosebud Valley Nature Preserve. There's not much to the structure—or to the haunted tale that goes along with it—but plenty of people certainly talk and write about the place.

Legend states that a young girl was playing at this spot when she died, and now her spirit is still there enjoying itself. The cause of death is uncertain; we don't even know if she died of natural causes, foul play, or an accident of some sort. But however she died it must not have been too bad since people claim to hear the ghostly girl laughing on the bridge. Her apparition has been glimpsed a few times, but most often it's just the spooky laugh that's experienced.

Nearby is an awesome preserve with lots to see and do. Maybe make the bridge just one stop in a day of exploring and enjoying nature.

## Morrison Bridge—Portland, Oregon

During the late 1700s, the Willamette River was a vast transportation way for those who dealt in the fur trade. Boats, large and small, would make their way along, selling their wares to various ports along the way. Perhaps the phantom rowboat that is now seen in the river is a remnant of this time.

If you ask Portlanders about their odd ghost you will get various descriptions of the boat (and the person doing the rowing), so dating the sighting is a bit difficult. They say he rows along, just minding his own business, and is oblivious of anyone watching.

Truth be told, the ghost is said to have been seen at various points along the Willamette within city limits, not just at this bridge. However, since this particular span accommodates pedestrian and bikes, I thought it would make the perfect perch to do some river watching.

The bridge was built in 1958 and is listed on the National Register of Historic Places, so it adds a second sight to your walking tour if the rowing specter refuses to show up for you. The city of Portland is known as one of the most haunted cities in America— and it offers several different haunted tours (including a haunted pub crawl). So there are plenty of paranormal attractions to keep you occupied while you visit here.

## Baltimore Pike Bridge—Chadds Ford, Pennsylvania

A book could be written about the history of the Brandywine Creek alone. Also known as the Brandywine River, this area was inhabited by the Lenape tribe of Native Americans prior to the arrival of European settlers in the early 1600s. Multiple wars between various Native American nations took place long before the infamous Battle of the Brandywine went down during the Revolutionary War in 1777, so there's been quite a lot of bloodshed in this area over the centuries. It's because of this that many say this stretch of road is haunted.

Sightings of phantom soldiers, ghostly horse-drawn wagons, and misty apparitions have been reported dozens of times—and it's generally well known (or at least well considered) that the Brandywine is haunted. In addition to the residual spirits wandering around, eyewitness accounts also include disembodied voices, the sounds of musket fire/battle, and odd mists that seem to move against the wind along the riverbank.

If you take a trip to this spot, consider stopping in the Brandywine River Museum nearby. The folks there know the history of the river and can probably tell you more ghost stories about Chadds Ford that you would enjoy.

## Sonestown Covered Bridge
## —Davidson Township, Pennsylvania

Built in 1850 over Muncy Creek, this beautiful structure is also known as the Davidson Covered Bridge. It has withstood numerous floods and been repaired/improved many times over the years and is yet standing. It was originally made for people to have access to nearby Johnny Hazen's Gristmill.

Today, the bridge cannot withstand heavy traffic (large trucks are diverted to nearby Veterans Memorial Bridge), but it can certainly handle a carload of ghost adventurers passing through. And why would you make this trip? To see the ghost of the Civil War soldier of course. For more than fifty years, locals have been telling yarns about the specter. He is supposed to be a soldier who marched off to war and was killed; now his spirit is trying to return home.

Investigators who live in the area say that it's actually easier to park your car on the road leading up to the span and watch the bridge from a few feet away. It is a tourist attraction, so people are quite accustomed to seeing pedestrians checking out the bridge. Happy hunting!

## Braddock's Run Bridge—Fayette County, Pennsylvania

Dating back to the French and Indian War, this bridge saw the march of General Braddock and British troops to their doom against the French and local Native Americans. Caught off guard as they crossed the bridge, the English troops were slaughtered as they attempted to rally late and fight back. Losses were high and Braddock himself would later succumb to his wounds.

Since that fateful day in 1755, people have spotted the ghost of a British soldier on the bridge. Legend says he still believes the bridge to be a dangerous place and will escort anyone who crosses it. The bridge crosses the Big Sandy Creek and there's some dispute regarding whether it is located on private property or not. Some say it's actually along the Sandy Creek Trail. If locating the bridge becomes a problem, consider day-tripping over to the Fort Necessity National Battlefield. They should be able to point out an exact location for the bridge—and there's more to learn there about the French and Indian War, General Braddock, and other historical curiosities. You can also check out General Braddock's grave.

## Crum Creek Bridge—Media, Pennsylvania

Known in ghost-hunting circles as the Dog Kennel Road Bridge, this small span is the site of a sad residual haunt. The spirit of a young girl is said to sit at the edge of the bridge, staring off into the distance. If approached, the ghost will ignore you until you get right next to her, and then she simply disappears. Technically, this bridge is on Paxon Hollow Road (Dog Kennel Road changes its name to Paxon Hollow Road just before the bridge), not far from Rose Tree Park between the towns of Media and Newtown Square.

The entire stretch of Dog Kennel Road is known for spooky stories involving apparitions, dark figures, and strange mists, so you may want to take a slow cruise along the entire, short stretch. You may also see a few confused ghost hunters wandering around; there are a few small bridges situated along the drive and many mistake them for the famous haunted one perched over Crum Creek.

## Colt State Park Bridge—Bristol, Rhode Island

Once a working farm back in the day, this state park has a plethora of activities for the outdoor enthusiast. It has bicycle trails, picnic areas, a view of Narragansett Bay, and the famous Chapel by the Sea. For the paranormal enthusiast, the park has a couple additional sights, too.

There are three ghosts that are regularly seen, and they seem to think they are still on the farm. First there's the spirit of a stable worker that is said to hang out in the park's office (it was, reportedly, a barn originally) and is sometimes seen just outside the building. Then there's a pair of ghostly girls who are thought to have drowned close to the beach. They've been seen on the trail leading to the beach and on this small bridge that is now part of a bike trail. Perhaps this trail leads to the beach? Eventually?

At any rate, the spirits seem harmless. The office ghost is said to even play pranks on those inside and the two female entities seem to do their own thing, ignoring anyone who notices them.

## Moosup River Bridge—Moosup Valley, Rhode Island

This historic district located in the town of Foster only has a few buildings scattered along Moosup Valley Road; there's the library, the old Moosup Valley Christian Church, and Grange Hall. All of these are in close vicinity of the bridge—a fact that is of importance when discussing the ghost that is seen here.

Who's the ghost? It appears to be the spirit of a man carrying a shovel. Locals say it's the same spirit that's been seen in the infamously haunted Grange Hall. Others say the entity is associated with nearby Tyler Cemetery. Either way, there have been a few sightings of the apparition on the bridge, sometimes accompanied by the sounds of digging, cold spots, and a mumbling voice that sounds like it is coming from beneath the span.

Historic towns tend to have the best ghost stories and this one sounds like a bit of a mystery. Why does the cemetery gravedigger haunt Grange Hall? Is there a reason the spirit rotates between these three locations? As mentioned, a library is nearby that probably has some knowledgeable historians working there. Do some Scooby-Doo-style work and figure it all out.

## Langham Creek Bridge—Houston, Texas

Legend states that a troop of soldiers from the American Civil War engaged in a skirmish at the location that is now known as Bear Creek Park (in the vicinity of this bridge). Apparently, they're still there. People have seen phantoms in uniform on the road and bridge that seem to be trudging along, oblivious to passersby. Well, almost oblivious. If you slow down when you see the specters and drive by slowly, witnesses say the ghosts will knock on your passing car.

There are no battles historically associated with this particular spot; however, loyalists from both sides would often take up arms and engage in small skirmishes all over the South, so it's not beyond reason that this would occur here. Since the ghosts are seen marching down the road, you might want to consider using the park as your base of operations. You can park there safely and stake out the road/bridge for the military spirits performing their ghostly parade.

## Thompson Island Bridge—San Marcos, Texas

There are actually two ghost stories about this bridge (and immediate area). The first concerns the ghost of a Confederate soldier who was guarding the bridge when he was shot and killed during the American Civil War. He was guarding the route to the cotton gin when he was hit, and it's said he's still standing on the bridge, unaware that he is now dead.

In addition to this, if you walk along the bank of the water below the span, you may encounter a La Llorona spirit of this area. It's said she was the widow of a Confederate officer; when she received word her husband had been killed in the war, things went very awry for her and her family. The money ran out and she was now without any means to support the household. Half crazy with poverty and sorrow, she went to the bridge and drowned her children there, sobbing the entire time. Now her spirit wanders, eternally regretful for the horrible act she did.

Between these two ghosts—and the wonderful historic sites that reside in this region—you should have a great time exploring here.

## Mountain Meadows Trail Bridge—St. George, Utah

The infamous slaughter of emigrants traveling to California by Mormon militiamen in 1857 is a terrible page in American history. After radical Mormons attacked a wagon train for passing through Utah territory, they deemed it necessary to eliminate all the witnesses, so they murdered more than 120 men, women, and children at this location. Only children under the age of seven were allowed to live. It would be years before one person would accept the burden of guilt for the deed and would be executed for it.

Today there is a memorial to mark this horrible event, and it should come as no surprise that the entire area is thought to be haunted by these tormented souls. The small bridge along the trail to the monument crosses the Magotsu Creek; after the slaughter of the families, it's said the water ran red with blood.

Disembodied voices, apparitions, and a pervading feeling of heaviness permeate this area. Soak in the history and keep your eyes open for the paranormal. This historic site is known for both.

## Float Bridge Road Bridge—Castleton, Vermont

Lake Bomoseen, where this particular bridge is located, is quite the tourist attraction in Vermont. It's part of Bomoseen State Park, along with campgrounds, hiking trails, and some of the best kayaking in the state. And while the bridge may be a great spot to keep a look out for the lake's ghosts, kayaking may be even better.

The story goes that three men were rowing across the lake to visit a favorite watering hole when they went missing. Presumed to be drunk, the men most likely capsized and drowned. Or at least that's what the locals assume. Since that fateful day, people have spotted the spectral rowboat pulling along in the water. While it seems that the ghosts can show up at any time on the lake (one witness actually claims to have seen the men/boat during the day), it's said your best odds are to watch for it on nights with a full moon. Maybe this was the setting the night the men went missing.

## Fauquier and Alexandria Turnpike Bridge —Manassas, Virginia

Also known as the Stone Bridge, this old structure dates back to 1825 and can be found close to the entrance of the Manassas National Battlefield Park. The American Civil War's impact on this area of Virginia cannot be understated; in the First Battle of Bull Run alone, there were almost five thousand casualties with more than eight hundred killed! It was the bloodiest battle in American history at that point. So it's no wonder that most of this battlefield is considered haunted.

Unlucky spirits that have found themselves forever wandering the location of their demise have been spotted throughout the park (and if you ask your tour guide about them, they are more than happy to point out some of the better spots for you). As for the bridge, people have seen the pale apparitions of soldiers marching across it. It's said you can tell when it is happening because the sounds of cannon fire will usually accompany the spectacle. Take a walk around this park and soak up the history—you never know what you're going to see in a place like this.

## 14th Street Long Bridge—Washington, DC

Dating back to 1903, this is one of five bridges that cross the Potomac River, connecting Arlington, Virginia, and the capitol. If you're looking at the bridges, this is the one that has railroad traffic—so don't cross it! Instead, check it out from nearby Ohio Drive.

This span is said to be the spot for a historical, residual haunting. General Edward Braddock launched his now famous Braddock Expedition from this spot in 1775, and it would end with the Battle of the Monongahela in Braddock, Pennsylvania. People say you can hear what sounds like horses galloping, people talking, guns firing, etc. Some have indicated that this is actually no haunting at all, but is a portal location that allows people to hear sounds (and sometimes see sights) from the past. Whatever the reason, don't be surprised if you hear some strange sounds while in this area.

## M Street Bridge—Washington, DC

Much like the previous listing for the 14th Street Bridge (and most of the other locations in Washington, DC), this location is haunted by a few different specters from the past. The first is said to be a phantom carriage, horses and all, that is seen speeding along the street and crossing the bridge. This act most likely dates back to the original wooden bridge that stood at this spot in 1788.

Along with this speeding apparition, people also see the ghost of a small drummer boy standing on the bridge. Also attributed to the Revolutionary War era, this spirit plays his instrument and ignores anyone who encounters him. Legend says he drowned after being knocked off the bridge during a parade/retinue that was making its way across.

Both of the Washington, DC, bridges listed in this chapter make an excellent start to a great haunted tour of the capitol. There are numerous haunted places in walking distance from this spot and many are worth taking the time to visit.

## Fort Laramie Bridge—Goshen County, Wyoming

This pedestrian bridge over the North Platte River makes for a great spot to catch one of the most unique haunted sights in the country: A ghost ship. This span dates back to 1875, and it was closed down to automobile traffic when a new bridge was built nearby in 1958. Now it's a popular place for a stroll—or to go watch for phantom ships.

Local legend says the mysterious boat has been seen since before the construction of this bridge. Accounts say that an odd fog will sweep over the river, seemingly from nowhere, then the pale ship (manned by the dead) will suddenly appear and move down the river. When the fog blows away, the ship goes with it.

It makes for a great story, but I would be remiss if I didn't tell you the darker side of this tale. Legend also states that sighting the ship is an omen of death—either for you or for someone close to you. So maybe you don't really want to see this spooky sight. Instead, take a nice historic tour of Fort Laramie and learn about the other haunted places in the area. Places that won't predict your doom.

## Chapter Six

# THE DEAD HITCHHIKER

When I think about phantom hitchhikers, I'm always reminded of one of the segments in the second *Creepshow* movie. In the film, a lady runs over a man who's hitching and then leaves him dead on the road. The angry spirit then proceeds to haunt and torture the woman all the way to her home. While there are no haunted places listed here that have a story specifically like this, there are certainly some spooky tales in this chapter.

The setting of driving alone at night on a desolate road, and spying the apparition of a lonely soul walking along, is enough to chill anyone. There aren't many of these ghostly pedestrians who like to hang out at bridges, but the examples I could find are all documented here. Enjoy!

## Second Creek Bridge—Elgin, Alabama

Where US Highway 72 crosses Second Creek in Alabama is a bridge with a peculiar story. It seems that during the 1930s (locals are a little foggy on the exact decade, but the details seem to point to the area of 1930 to 1950), there was a jazz man walking to the city of Florence.

His trip was cut short, however, when he was struck and killed by a passing motorist on this bridge.

Now, according to legend, the occasional driver will encounter the ghost as he is crossing the span. If you pick up the spectral hitchhiker, he will ask you to take him to Florence and then begin talking about his trumpet. Of course, somewhere between Second Creek and Florence the phantom disappears.

The man is simply known locally as the Jazz Man because of his reference to a trumpet and due to the fact he is said to appear wearing an old, white zoot suit. And it's because of these assorted clues that most people date the dead man back to the 1930s. If you see the ghost crossing this bridge, have no fear. He won't stick around long in or out of your car.

## Bob Graham Sunshine Skyway Bridge —Tampa Bay, Florida

With a total length of 21,877 feet, and stretching some 180 feet in the air over the waters below, the Skyway Bridge has had a tragic history. The original version of this structure opened in 1954 to the public—and aside from the occasional jumper—suffered nothing too out of the ordinary for a span of this size. Then in 1980 disaster struck. It was during a thunderstorm that year that the ship *Summit Venture* ran into a support column beneath the bridge. It caused a collapse that dumped six cars, a truck, and a Greyhound bus into the bay. That day, thirty-five people died. This, in itself, would be enough to justify a haunting at this place, but it's sad to say the story gets even worse.

In 1987, the current version of the bridge opened. Since the opening of the new bridge, more than two hundred people have committed suicide at the Skyway. This is despite constant surveillance by the highway patrol and the prohibition of stopped vehicles, bicycles, and pedestrians.

The most well-known ghost story about this bridge involves the ghost of a young woman. Those who have seen her say she walks the bridge, agitated, until someone stops and picks her up. Once she is in the vehicle, she appears even more upset—wringing her hands, crying, etc.—until she finally disappears before the bridge is fully crossed. It's also worth noting that, in addition to the phantom hitchhiker, many claim to see the ghostly image of the Greyhound bus scooting along the road.

## Metropolitan Avenue Bridge—Atlanta, Georgia

In the realm of ghost stories there are several different types of tales. The most common would fall under the heading of urban legend— and the yarn about this particular bridge is definitely that. But before we dive into the story, it should be noted that this location isn't a bridge per se. It's a set of train tracks crossing over Metropolitan Avenue (and the tracks don't really even qualify as being a trestle of any kind). We don't have to be concerned about that, however, since the ghost in question is said to appear under the tracks, by the road.

The legend goes like this: If you happen along the road at night you may notice a young girl hitchhiking at this spot. Pick her up and she will give you a local address to take her to. While she is in the car, it's said that she will not speak and that she always looks straight ahead through the windshield. Once you arrive at your destination the girl will tell you, "Thanks for the ride," get out of the car, and promptly disappear.

To go the extra mile with the story, you can supposedly then go to the front door of the residence you are at and give it a knock. You will be told by the inhabitant there that the young girl used to live in the home, but she was killed in an auto accident at the spot you picked her up. Since nobody has actually noted this address, it can probably be assumed this story is simply a legend. But on the off chance you run into the girl and give her a ride, be sure to let all of us know where she lives.

## 16th Avenue Bridge—Kaimuki, Hawaii

The whole idea of eternally looking for a ride, getting a ride, and then ending right back where you started is a sort of hell in itself. When it happens to the spirit of a little girl … well, it becomes particularly tragic. Such is the case with this bridge in Kaimuki.

It's said a young girl was struck and killed in a hit-and-run accident—and now people see her spirit wandering the bridge at night. Witnesses claim that they have stopped to ask the girl if she's okay, if she needs a ride, etc. Then the girl climbs into the car and rides until the end of the bridge. At that point she simply disappears.

This haunting has been reported an incredible amount of times, and those who claim to have had this exact event happen to them keep piling up. If you find yourself driving on the island of Oahu it may be worth your time to take a trip to this location and give it a whirl. If nothing else, it sounds like a rather tame haunt and you'd certainly have a rather unique vacation story.

## Edna Collins Bridge—Greencastle, Indiana

Though the ghost at this location isn't technically hitchhiking, this chapter seemed the best fit for this particular bridge and story. The Edna Collins Bridge was built in 1922 over Little Walnut Creek. And it's said that the bridge's spiritual namesake, Edna Collins, was a little girl who loved to go swimming at this spot. The daily ritual (when it was warm enough to go swimming) was for Edna's parents to drop her off at the creek, let her swim for a spell, and then come back for her. They would pull their car up and honk three times, signaling little Edna to come to the car. Well, one day she didn't come when they honked. She had drowned in the creek.

So the legend goes that if you now park on this bridge and honk your horn three times, the spirit of little Edna will come to your car and maybe even crawl inside. In addition to this, people have claimed to see the small ghost playing in the water and to find childlike handprints on their car after visiting the bridge. As a bizarre side note, there is a spin-off tale that concerns the death of the girl's mother; some say that the mother, distraught after Edna's death, hung herself in a church that's nearby. Because of this, her apparition is also included in many of the eyewitness accounts from here.

## Hamilton Road Bridge—Mulberry, Indiana

The bridge on this stretch of road heads a trio of urban legends that teenagers have been testing for decades. But if you want to check it out, first you need to make sure you are at the correct bridge. There are actually three spans along Hamilton Road and you will want to visit the third structure to kick off your night of legend tripping.

*Legend 1:* If you stop before crossing the bridge in question, and then flash your headlights four times, you will see a man suddenly appear behind your vehicle and start chasing you across the bridge. He is supposedly the ghost of a hitchhiker who was struck and killed at that spot.

*Legend 2:* A bit farther up the same road you will see a small graveyard. If you park here and watch the woods, you will see phantom flames leap up. Legend says a church burned at this spot during the 1800s, killing all the parishioners inside. If you wait long enough, you can now see that moment in time reenacted.

*Legend 3:* After you leave the graveyard and drive a bit more, there is a set of railroad tracks crossing the road. If you stop on the tracks (not a smart move to make since trains do come through here), it's said you will hear a train sound its whistle and see lights coming down the tracks—but there will be no train. To top it all off, after you leave, if you check your car's bumper there will be handprints on it. It seems a young man died after being struck by a train on those tracks and now he attempts to push people clear of them. (See, parking on train tracks is a bad idea!)

## Child's Creek Bridge—Closplint, Kentucky

Not much is known about this small bridge on the outskirts of the unincorporated town of Closplint. Locals tell the story of a young woman who perished in an accident at this location and who now haunts the area here. While she may not have been a hitchhiker when she died, most who catch a glimpse of her as they hit the bridge mistake her for one. It's too bad, though, that most people only get one good look at the apparition.

Apparently, seeing this spirit causes drivers to duplicate the demise of the young woman; a wreck usually happens after she is seen. While the original death at this location cannot be verified, it does appear that there have been an inordinate amount of auto accidents in this area—though it may or may not have anything to do with a ghost. If you decide to test the theory and go hunting for this particular specter, you may want to drive very slowly; at least you may then survive any kind of accident you have while gawking at the dead.

## Charles Burr Lane Bridge—Opelousas, Louisiana

This well-hidden spot is a popular high school dare in the area. The bridge is tiny, but the story is big. It also has a bizarre twist on the typical dead hitchhiker legend. It's said that if you drive this road at night you will notice an old man walking along in the area of the bridge. You will know it is the correct old man if he is carrying a pale green, glowing lantern. If you stop to ask the old man if he needs a ride, he will disappear. However, if you drive past him, you will suddenly sense a dark presence in your vehicle. Apparently at this point a black mass, in the vague shape of a human being, will appear in your backseat. It will remain there until you attempt to touch it or stop your car.

There's not much info regarding the relationship of these two apparitions. Are they the same being? Are they two different people who were killed at this location? Nobody knows. It's a creepy tale that takes place on a spooky stretch of road. Take a drive down into the Louisiana country and check it out for yourself.

## Upper Blackwell Road Bridge—Blackwell, Missouri

Spanning the Big River, this bridge (as well as the road) has had quite the reputation over the years. Generally regarded as a location where bad things tend to happen, most people in the area simply say the spot is evil. There are a couple stories associated with the region, with the most well known involving a phantom pair of hitchhikers who are seen leading up to the bridge.

Reportedly, the hitchhikers will flag you down but disappear when you actually stop. Then there are the stories involving a mysterious car that will appear if you flash your headlights three times as you are crossing the bridge. Both of these tales are supposed to be the result of a car accident that occurred in the 1950s. If all this isn't enough, there are also the legends told about a hanging judge that was infamous in the old days. If you did wrong, he would sentence you to death and then you were dragged to old Black Tram (as the first version of the bridge at this spot was known) and strung up. Because of these killings, people now feel like there is an ugly, evil presence on the bridge.

Witnesses say disembodied voices are common, as well as the feeling of being watched. Sound spooky? Then I probably shouldn't add that people have also seen dark figures standing on the bridge.

## Broad River Bridge—Caroleen, North Carolina

This rather plain, concrete bridge spanning Broad River is on US-221 ALT on the south side of town. Since it doesn't have any over-hanging structure (just a simple metal railing beside the road), it's rather easy to drive right over it without ever knowing you were on it! Of course, you might have a hint you're on the haunted bridge if you see a pair of elderly, female apparitions walking along the road.

The story goes that, if you pick the pair up, they will say nothing but will get in your vehicle and ride along for a bit. Then they disappear. It has been supposed that they died in a vehicle accident either by driving off the bridge or somewhere else nearby and then they wandered to the bridge in the afterlife. However they got there, those who have picked up the ghosts say the experience is rather unsettling.

Once they are in your vehicle—and the eerie silence ensues—that slow, creeping dread of the uncanny hits you. Then, when the lack of interaction from the women becomes unbearable, they fade away right before your eyes. Sound scary? Go find out. Just don't miss the bridge.

## Lydia's Bridge—Jamestown, North Carolina

This underpass/bridge is the setting for one of North Carolina's most famous ghost stories. It's an almost certain bet that if the subject of hauntings is brought up, somebody is going to tell you about the sad hitchhiker who is known as Lydia.

Here's the story: If you drive along High Point Road (US-70A) toward the span in question, you will see a young woman in a white dress waving at you to stop. She will get in your car and explain that her name is Lydia and that she is trying to get home from her school dance. She will give you some directions, but on the way to her house she will disappear. Supposedly, one person actually managed to get all the way to her home before she vanished. When he went to the front door of the place, an elderly woman greeted him and explained the girl was her daughter, who had died in an auto accident after leaving a local dance.

It's said this accident occurred sometime in the 1920s or 1930s, so the encounter at the girl's home must have also happened some time ago. A haunted tour of North Carolina would not be complete without a visit to this spot—and the story has certainly been featured a number of times on television and in books. And here it is again!

## Main Street Bridge—Pawtucket, Rhode Island

The sad apparition that's seen walking across this old bridge (it dates back to 1858 and is thought to be the oldest highway bridge in current use in Rhode Island) is less of a hitchhiker and more like a ghost that's usually mistaken for a hitchhiker. It's said that when motorists see the spirit on the bridge, they pull over and ask him if he needs a ride—and then the man disappears.

This area is sort of known for hauntings, so this story doesn't really come as a surprise; nearby is the Slater Mill historic site that has ghosts of its own. The mill's spooky inhabitants are said to be the unfortunate workers who were killed while working in this Industrial Revolution era textile factory. Many of these lost souls are even said to be children. Apparitions, moans/cries, and dark figures are the most commonly reported activity in the mill.

Maybe the bridge spirit is a former worker who decided to quit because of the working conditions there. I'd definitely try to hit both of these sites if you're planning a paranormal trip to the town of Pawtucket.

## Gervais Street Bridge—Columbia, South Carolina

Built in 1928, this concrete arch bridge is the third to stand at this spot over the Congaree River. The first dates back to 1827; it was burned down during the American Civil War by Confederate troops to slow the march of General Sherman into the South. The second was constructed in 1870 and was the only bridge across this river at the time. The remains of both of these can be seen from the current bridge. But I'm sure you're more interested in seeing the ghost at this spot.

It's said the spirit of a young girl can be seen hitchhiking here. She appears to be wearing garb from the 1940s or 1950s and will get in your car if you actually stop to pick her up. However, she won't speak or respond to any questions, such as, "Where are you headed?" Before you get to the end of the bridge she will disappear. According to one of her chauffeurs, as he was driving her across the bridge he noticed that his car was getting colder and colder—and at one point he thought she appeared as a black, blurry thing sitting in the seat. Kind of adds a spooky spin to the story, doesn't it?

## Wateree River Bridge—Laurens County, South Carolina

Located along US Highway 76, this bridge crosses a swampy area of South Carolina that is already known for being rather scary. But when you add in this ghostly tale, the westbound portion of this bridge kicks it up a notch!

The story goes that a couple was returning home to Columbia when they noticed a young woman walking in the rain along this bridge. They stopped and picked her up. When they asked where the girl was going, she said she was going home to Columbia. The couple offered to take her home and began driving. A few miles down the road, they attempted to make conversation with the girl, but to their dismay, she evaporated right before their eyes. Passersby now claim to see the spirit of this girl regularly on the bridge.

A second version of the tale exists—one that's a bit more limited and specific. In this iteration the girl only appears on the anniversary of her death, and when the original couple picked her up, she told them that she lived on a particular street in Columbia. After the girl disappeared, the couple decided to visit the address the ghost had given them. They found an elderly woman at the address who appeared to be expecting them; she informed the couple that her daughter always appears and catches a ride with someone on the anniversary of her death. Since we don't know who the girl is, or when she died, it makes it a bit difficult to be at the bridge on that day.

## West 26th Street Bridge—Sioux Falls, South Dakota

This small overpass crossing Interstate 29 (I-29) is known for being the home of two phantom joggers running along the road. Those who have seen the ghosts say that they ignore cars passing by and seem to go about their business, oblivious to everything around them. One encounter, however, does detail an attempt to give the joggers a ride; this witness said that he pulled up beside the spirits because he thought they looked distressed. But when he asked them if they were alright and if they needed a ride, they faded away before his eyes.

While this spot may be known for these ghosts, it's also known as a popular place to debunk a ghost story. There are at least four pages online that detail reasons why this spot is not haunted. Some of these explanations are even more ludicrous than the story of the haunting. If you want to find out if the haunting is real or not, you will have to go see for yourself.

## Provo Canyon Road Bridge—Bridal Veil Falls, Utah

The bridge crossing Lost Creek is entirely unnoticeable; it's simply part of the road with some simple guardrails. But if you catch a glimpse of the famous ghost that's seen along this route, I'm sure you will notice that.

The spirit is a female who is seen dressed in white, hitchhiking along this road. It's said she was driving either to or from her wedding when she drove off the road here and perished. The lone witness to the event said that her veil was still floating in the wind when her car hurtled through the air.

Witnesses say your best bet for seeing the apparition is in the early morning hours. Since most accounts say she appears as a normal person (not a ghost), you may want to take notice of any woman in a bridal gown walking in this area. Chances are she will be a ghost.

While you're here, you may also want to take a moment to absorb the awesome scenery; the 607-foot-tall waterfall that's nearby is quite the sight to see.

## 5th Street Bridge—Huntington, West Virginia

This bridge, along with the entire stretch of 5th Street, is known for being the stomping grounds of a female ghost. First reported in the local newspaper in 1942, the article states that a Black and White Cab driver encountered a girl hailing him for a ride on 5th Street Hill. She gave him a destination and they talked as they drove along; he thought it was odd that she wasn't wearing a coat in winter. When they reached the end of the drive, the cabbie turned for the fare and the girl had disappeared.

Since then, this story makes the papers periodically with a new sighting. And it seems that drivers in the region are still seeing the young apparition looking for a ride. In some instances she has been said to disappear while crossing the bridge and others say she only fades away after you arrive at an address in West Huntington. Either way, your best bet to see this ghost seems to be driving a taxi. Good luck with that.

## Jay Road Bridge—Boltonville, Wisconsin

Known to locals as Seven Bridges Road, this stretch through the countryside of Wisconsin has several bridges along it. You can pick which one you want to visit since the entire road is said to be haunted!

There are two basic stories that legend trippers point to when visiting this spot. The first involves the apparition of a lady that people see jogging along the road. Of course, nobody realizes she is a ghost until they stop to ask her if she needs a ride. Then it's pretty obvious she is dead when she suddenly disappears.

The second story is an odd one. It's said that an old house that once stood along the road burned one night, killing a woman and all her cats. Now the apparition of the woman is seen wandering along in the areas off the road, a stop sign now bleeds, and corpses of cats turn up a lot. See, I told you it was weird. Nobody has any idea why a stop sign would bleed in this scenario, but there it is— the legend of Seven Bridges Road.

## Chapter Seven
# SCARY CREATURES

A haunting is not the only paranormal event that can occur on or around bridges. Tales of frightening monsters, bizarre creatures, and unexplained events are also told from time to time. Cryptozoology is the study of forgotten animals—sometimes these are animals that are long extinct, sometimes they are the things of legend that many say have never existed. Bigfoot, the Loch Ness Monster, and Mothman are examples of such creatures.

This chapter is for the crypto junkies of the world. Bridges that are the stomping grounds for legendary beasts make up these tales. This could be one of the scarier sections of this book; ghosts on most occasions do not harm people, but what about a demon dog or a hairy biped (more commonly known as a Sasquatch)? Be cautious when visiting these locales. Sometimes the truth is, indeed, out there. And sometimes it is quite frightening.

## Tilly Willy Bridge—Fayetteville, Arkansas

The story told about this bridge is unique in a couple of different ways. First off, the bridge in question is gone—it was demolished for safety reasons. But that hasn't stopped activity from occurring at the spot where it once stood. Second, in addition to having an odd entity that reputedly hangs out in the vicinity, the bridge also has a ghost story associated with it.

The haunting is pretty straightforward. Sometime during the 1970s, a young woman was driving home with her kids when her car went off the bridge, killing them all (some locals will tell you there were actually two accidents of this variety here). Some say it was a deliberate murder/suicide; some say it was a pure accident. Either way, the spirit of the woman has been witnessed on the bridge and in the fields nearby. She is seen wearing a white dress.

However, if you visit this location along Wilson Hollow Road, you may see more than just a ghost … It seems that a pair of ghost hunters were checking out Tilly Willy Bridge in the 1990s when they saw something quite unexpected: A green goblin. Not the Marvel Comics bad guy—an actual green creature skulking about the area. They, of course, fled in fear.

Since then, others have reported seeing the exact same thing. Most believe the thing is an inhuman spirit that's drawn to the bridge because of the associated deaths. Or could it be an actual goblin of some kind? Go and see for yourself …

## Creek Road Bridge—Ojai, California

Just north of Camp Comfort County Park, a two-lane bridge is on Creek Road that crosses the San Antonio Creek. This bridge—as well as the entire area surrounding Camp Comfort—has a ridiculous amount of ghost stories associated with it. People have seen the ghost of a bloody bride, the spirit of a decapitated motorcyclist, and even the multiple apparitions of a group of children that were reputedly killed in a school bus accident. But all of these stories pale in comparison to the tales that surround two bizarre creatures that are seen in the vicinity of this bridge.

The first of these bizarre creatures is known as Char Man. He appears as a severely burnt man/thing with charred skin that will attack you if you dare to stop on the bridge and yell into the nearby woods for him (some say you have to yell for help). No one is sure where the legend of Char Man comes from, but most say he was once a man that was burned to death—either in a forest fire or a horrible car accident. The story of Char Man is so prevalent in this area that many even call the bridge "Char Man Bridge." But, man or demon, he is not alone...

In addition to the ghosts and Char Man, there is also a vampire. In all versions of the tale of the Ojai Vampire, the creature is said to have immigrated to the area in the late 1800s. Shortly after his arrival, locals began to become suspicious of the odd new neighbor when he was never seen during the day and cattle started turning up drained of blood. It all came to a head when a posse was formed and the vampire's tomb was found. Though the tomb is said to have been guarded by a massive black dog, the group managed to repel the beast and find the vampire within. Now is where the story splits... In one version, the vampire was staked and slain. In the other, the vampire rose from the tomb and fled into the setting sun.

People have attempted to find the old tomb numerous times over the years to no avail. Maybe you'll have better luck.

## Santa Ana River Bridge—Riverside, California

The circumstances concerning this particular story may seem familiar; apparently two different men by the name of Wetzel witnessed strange creatures in 1958. We are only concerned with the Wetzel who lived in Riverside. This sighting happened one evening when

Charles Wetzel was approaching the Santa Ana River Bridge in his car. According to the legend, he was about to cross the span when a giant, reptilian creature approached him and began attacking his car. Frightened beyond belief, Wetzel managed to shake the creature from his vehicle, where he quickly ran it over. He then went to the local police station and made a report about the entire incident (presumably this is how we still know the tale today).

Since then, people have spoken often of the Riverside Monster, and, on occasion, have even seen the thing. Since 1958, several locals have reported having encounters with the creature either on the bridge or below it in the area surrounding the riverbed (it is presumed that the riverbed is actually closer to the original incident that happened in 1958 since the bridge is a replacement of an older one). It's said the thing will leave behind a green residue after it attacks a vehicle.

Though I managed to only find one account of the monster attacking anyone, anything is possible. Take a trip to Riverside and do some exploring...but be careful!

## Hopyard Road Bridge—East Haddam, Connecticut

When the subject of scary creatures is being discussed, there are perhaps none as frightening as the devil himself. And that's who is said to walk the infamous Devil's Hopyard State Park. The original tale concerning Satan at this location involves him sitting on a lone boulder that's perched at the top of Chapman Falls. He's said to often hang out there and play the fiddle. But that's only the beginning of the story. The entire park is said to be haunted by the demonic spirits that accompany the devil. Witnesses have heard evil laughter in the trees, seen bizarre entities, and claimed to have had vaguely humanlike mists follow them.

Along Hopyard Road is trio of historic bridges that date back to 1937—and this stretch seems to be a favorite of the evil spirits that are said to roam the park. According to at least two witnesses, the area surrounding the bridges is the most active. Balls of glowing light, paranormal mists, and even dark voices have been heard on the bridges—and, indeed, all along Hopyard Road. While this haunting may have a sinister edge to it, people who live in the area say the spirits are harmless and simply want to get a scare out of those who are trespassing on their territory.

## Judith Road Bridge—Hartly, Delaware

As you make the drive along this dark road, you will want to keep an eye out for a small bridge skirted on both sides by a strip of trees. It seems a nondescript place—almost too simple to have so many spooky stories associated with it. Investigators that live in the area, as well as thrill seekers, tell quite a few tales about this old bridge and the environs that surround it.

First off, the spirit of a young girl is seen in the area. She's said to be associated with a haunted home that's nearby, and she's known to appear on the road approaching the bridge, as well as standing in nearby fields. Then there are the whispers and voices that many have heard coming from the forest just off the road—otherworldly voices that frighten anyone who hears them. And then there's the creature …

Sounding like an infamous black dog from legend, the huge beast is said to stalk the road and bridge and has been seen by numerous people. Those who've had a glimpse say the thing is terrifying and that it appears as a massive canine usually silhouetted against a distant light. Thankfully, those who have had the unfortunate experience of seeing the thing approach them say that it typically disappears before actually attacking.

## Brooks Bridge—Fort Walton Beach, Florida

Stories of the bizarre—and the paranormal—are often linked together. Such is the strange legend that involves this particular location. The Brooks Bridge was recently renovated to extend the life of this circa 1965 structure, so it should still be standing if you decide to check it out. Just be warned: You have to visit on the third Wednesday of the month at exactly midnight if you want to see the spirits here. You have to look at the water beneath the bridge.

And what will you see? Well, according to witnesses, you will see a group of ghostly wolves running across Santa Rosa Sound. Yes, you read that correctly—ghost wolves. People say the entities appear dark and blurry as they scamper along the waves, and that the phenomenon lasts about a minute. Now, with a story this strange you would think there would only be a single witness—maybe two—who tell this bizarre tale. You would be wrong. Locals say that many people have seen this event, and that the bridge draws a regular crowd on the evenings in question.

## Holland Road Bridge—Hawkinsville, Georgia

Some stories are frightening, some stories are bizarre, and some stories are both. Such is the case of Pigman's Bridge. If you wind along the long stretch of back country that lines Holland Road, you will eventually come across this bridge. Tales of the horrors surrounding this area are very well known in the area, so if you can't find the place just ask a local. Once you do find it, you have to ask yourself if you want to stick around. When night falls, you may not want to see something as horrific as the thing that's described here.

The Pigman has two background stories, each of them quite terrible. The tamest version of the tale involves a circus trainer who had an act that involved pigs—and when he retired from the entertainment business he decided to live under the bridge. But he couldn't do away with his pigs. So he cared for them until the day they broke free from their pens and ate the poor man alive.

The second version of the story omits the circus and simply characterizes the old man as a reclusive hermit who lived off pigs. He didn't want people coming around and bothering him, so he would place pig heads on stakes to ward off the curious. Eventually a nosy individual got a little too close to the guy, so he murdered the visitor and placed his head on a stake, too. Townies heard of the killing and stormed the old man, slaying him on the bridge.

In both legends, once the Pigman was dead, his spirit decided to stick around. These days he's seen on the bridge by those unfortunate enough to come across him. Sometimes he appears as the grizzly, old man; sometimes he's the horrible spirit of a man with a pig's head.

## Blood's Point Bridge—Belvidere, Illinois

An entire book could be written just about the legends concerning Blood's Point Road. There is a haunted cemetery where people say misty figures walk at night, tales of phantom vehicles driving along the road, and even a mysterious barn that's said to appear (and disappear) at random. Then there's the bridge.

Stories about this structure are quite varied as well. It's said a bus once wrecked on the bridge, killing all on board, and now you can have your car pushed along by the spirits there. Parking by the bridge will also expose you to possible apparitions and the sounds of voices talking and whistling. But, perhaps, the oddest story of all is that of Beulah the Witch.

During the days of Arthur Blood—one of the founders of the area and the namesake of this road—it's said he was plagued by the witch.

His children claimed to see her under the bridge and said that she was able to conjure fire from her fingers. Legend says the witch would then go on to slowly drive the Blood family mad, eventually culminating with several suicides on the bridge by hanging. Other bizarre whispers about Beulah also include her murdering her own children, conjuring hellhounds that still patrol the area today, and still appearing on the bridge as a dark entity with glowing red eyes.

## Bear Creek Bridge—Christian County, Illinois

Since I'm including evil witches as creatures, this chapter is a fitting place for this story. The circa 1916 truss bridge over Bear Creek is famous for thrill seekers—and along with nearby Anderson Cemetery, it makes for an interesting haunted location. As for the bridge, it's said that it's haunted due to the hanging of an old witch on the structure. Somehow a nearby stone house is involved—either the witch was a young girl who was from the place, or the witch magically made those in the house go crazy and kill each other (much like the Blood's Point Bridge tale).

Whichever version of the witch you prefer, witnesses say the bridge is the spot the spirit of the witch likes to haunt. People see her hanging from the bridge, hear mysterious voices, and encounter a massive black figure that seems to hover about the structure. Others have reported seeing glowing balls of light floating about and claim that the spirits from the cemetery will often be seen walking from there to the bridge.

If you go over to the cemetery, be wary; you may want permission to be there at night. Once you secure your way inside, be on the lookout for the woman in black who is said to walk there. You might also want to take a trip around the perimeter; a new area is supposed to magically materialize when the sun sets that's even more haunted.

## Ceylon Covered Bridge—Adams County, Indiana

Sounding like the foundation of a horror movie, the stories surrounding this particular haunted bridge fall firmly in the realm of urban legend—but that doesn't make visiting the spot any less frightening. Of course, the word *frightening* would only apply if you visit at night. During the day, this circa 1879 covered bridge is quite gorgeous.

Located on the outskirts of the town of Ceylon, this tourist stop is a popular dare for local high school students. Legend states that a group of teens once performed a séance on the bridge for fun—and all was, indeed, fun until one of their members fell over dead (some say the body was actually hanging from the bridge and that it fell during the séance). Since that night, the bridge has apparently become a portal to the netherworld.

People claim to hear hellish screams and see things that can only be described as demons. In addition to this, witnesses have also described evil black dogs standing in the road, misty apparitions floating about the area, and spooky laughter emanating from the bridge. If you visit, keep an eye out for teenagers—one of them just might jump out and do all the scaring.

## Old Railroad Bridge—Columbus, Indiana

Like most train trestles, this bridge should only be approached with caution and staked out from afar. Do not attempt to actually cross this bridge. It is not safe! The first challenge in checking out this haunted location is actually finding it, though. Located near Noblitt Park, this dilapidated structure crosses the Flatrock River—and is said to be guarded by a bizarre creature with glowing yellow eyes. It's unsure how, exactly, this thing came to be on this bridge.

There is a ghost story about a woman who leaped from the bridge with an infant—people claim to have seen the spirit of the lady and to have heard the cries of the baby. But there doesn't seem to be any clear connection between the creature and the haunting. Paranormal investigators have captured some great evidence at this spot and one group claims that the evil deed of the woman (killing her baby) is what brought the demon that now patrols this area into the world.

If you don't feel like hiking to a rickety bridge to possibly see a ghost or monster, you may want to get permission to visit the nearby park at night. Passersby claim to see the two anomalies there, too.

## 5th Road Bridge—Marshall County, Indiana

Snuggled between the towns of Bremen and Plymouth, this small bridge crosses the Yellow River along 5th Road. It's just down the road from another popular haunted spot in Indiana, the Little Egypt Cemetery. Also known as the Ewald Cemetery, this place is a popular locale for ghost watching and has its own collection of interesting ghost stories—including a phantom farmer, a ghostly baby crying in the night, and spirits that like to touch your car when you park in the vicinity.

As for the bridge, it is the stomping grounds of your everyday, run-of-the-mill troll. Yep, that's right—a troll. According to several witnesses, this seven- to nine-foot-tall creature likes to hang out around the Yellow River and is often spotted on the bridge, as well as underneath it.

Those who have been fortunate (or unfortunate?) enough to see the thing say it will throw stones and yell at anyone who gets too close, and that it will even give chase if you stick around long enough. If you manage to make the trip out into Marshall County to hunt the troll, be sure to take a camera. I would certainly like to see what this thing looks like.

## Old Kankakee River Bridge—San Pierre, Indiana

So a couple things about this particular haunting should be mentioned up front. One, the bridge is no longer standing—reports say there are simply concrete support columns marking the spot where this bridge once stood. Second, do not visit this location alone. Besides the spooky stories associated with this area, there is a very real criminal element that has been known to visit here. You may also want someone else along with you after you hear the legend of ... Dog Face Bridge!

The story goes like this ... A couple was on their way home when they started crossing the bridge one night. Suddenly, a dog ran in front of their vehicle. They hit the dog, then swerved off the bridge into the river below. Everyone was killed, but when the aftermath was searched, the dog and the woman in the car had been decapitated. And to make matters worse, the head of the dog and the body of the woman were not found at all.

Now it's said that the bizarre apparition of a woman with a dog's head is seen in the area around the old bridge. People claim to see the creature, hear ungodly growls and howls in the night, and to have even been chased by the thing. If you ask people in San Pierre about the story, you will get an earful. Every unexplained death in the region has been attributed to the Dog Face Lady.

## Skunk River Bridge—Metz, Iowa

Is this a twisted tale designed to frighten people or a bizarre ghost story? That seems to be the real question when one looks at the details of this odd haunting. The bridge that crosses the Skunk River along Neptune Street is said to be the hangout of a creature known locally as the Mud Monster of Metz or, sometimes, Mud Man.

Legend states the thing was created after an accident that caused a man to drown/suffocate in the mud below the bridge. Most believe the story was created to scare teenagers away from the river (it seems this is a popular make-out spot), but some say the thing is real—and many have claimed to have seen the monster wandering the river and even stalking the bridge itself.

Odd photos and video have captured a dark, vaguely manlike being around this area. The only eyewitness account I found online stated that the Mud Monster doesn't like anyone invading his territory and that he will chase you if you linger. Just be careful he doesn't chase you to the nearby Sugar Grove Cemetery. It, too, has quite a few ghostly tales uttered about it. And who wants to deal with a Mud Man *and* a ghost?

## Taylorsville Road Trestle—Fisherville, Kentucky

No chapter on creature-infested bridges would be complete without the bizarre tale of the Pope Lick Monster. But before jumping into the strange story of this mysterious Goat Man, it should be noted that this old train bridge is quite dilapidated and extremely dangerous. Spooky things aside, more than one unlucky person has lost their footing on this structure and tumbled to their demise, so watch for the monster from afar—do not attempt to get on the actual train tracks or trestle.

Now, the details of this particular case make for quite an interesting read. Being half goat and half man, most say the thing was part of a traveling circus that managed to escape from a train that passed through the area. Others say it is something supernatural entirely, and that it shouldn't be toyed with. Actually, everyone believes it probably shouldn't be toyed with.

Reputedly, sightings of the Goat Man started at the turn of the 1900s, became frequent during the 1940s and 1950s, faded for a while, and have now surged again. People say it lives somewhere under the trestle, but it will become infuriated with those who invade its home, often chasing people down the train tracks. Those who have been unfortunate enough to actually see the beast say it is horrifying—almost a demon-looking thing in the flesh. Your best bet to go looking for it would be along Taylorsville Road leading up to the tracks. But, again, do not attempt to walk the trestle. The area doesn't need ghosts in addition to the monster.

## Cody Road RR Bridge—Independence, Kentucky

The story of Pig Face is an odd one, with a bit of history involved to boot. During the days of prohibition, this area of Kentucky was rife with moonshiners. Moonshiners who had fierce rivalries to produce and sell the best (and most) white lightning. Because of this, violent acts were commonplace then. Pig Face is said to be the product of this era.

The story goes that one shiner decided to burn down the house of a rival, but he didn't realize there was a woman inside. She was killed, but she never left. Soon after the horrible act, shiners running their wares started to notice a woman with an odd face walking along the tracks. When she was approached, she would disappear. Tales, as well as sightings, of Pig Face have persisted ever since.

Interestingly, there is another version of the story that states Pig Face was struck and killed by a train, and that is the reason her face is messed up.

If you decide to hunt out this specter, know that you do not have to actually mess with the bridge itself. The bridge is actually a train trestle that crosses Cody Road. You can park below it and stake out the tracks for the spirit. One word of warning: Below the road is actually a creek. You will notice there are gates that block off the creek during flooding. If these gates are closed, or if you notice the water is high, don't linger. This spot is known for flash floods and people have been washed away in the past.

## Acton Lane Bridge—Charles County, Maryland

This bridge shares a story with a second bridge—Governor's Bridge listed in the crybaby bridge chapter of the book. They are both visited by a creature known locally as the Goat Man. This bizarre beast has been featured on many television programs and is one of the most well-known legends in the area.

The story goes that a scientist was working at the Beltsville Agricultural Research Center on experiments involving goats when something went awry. He became a half man, half goat abomination. If that wasn't bad enough, the transformation also caused him to become an ax-wielding maniac. And now the Goat Man spends his time wandering the countryside attacking cars, and whatever else he can find, with his weapon of choice.

Sightings date back to the 1950s, with most of them occurring at the nearby Lover's Lane or at this bridge. It's said that if you visit this spot at night and park for a while, you will begin to hear a grunting/snorting sound coming from Mattawoman Creek below you. It is, of course, the Goat Man. And he's probably coming for you. If you want to avoid such an encounter (ax-made dents are going to be hard to explain to your auto insurer), think about making the trip here during the day. You can always hunt for goat prints along the creek…

## Dice Road Bridge—Hemlock, Michigan

While a warlock isn't necessarily a creature, it feels like this bridge belongs in this section. Scary oddities seem to be the routine when people decide to go legend tripping at this now famous haunted bridge. Located just down the way from a cemetery (which is also known for its spooky sightings and tales), people claim to see a dark figure roaming the area that is thought to be the aforementioned warlock. It's said he became enraged after three girls mistakenly trampled his wife's grave, so he took them to the bridge and hung them.

In addition to sightings of the wizard, people have heard the screams of the girls in the night, as well as other odd voices that seemingly speak from right beside you as you are walking Dice Road. This could have something to do with the other stories about the area. The cemetery was, reputedly, the site of Satanic rituals and many claim that it was frequented by an insane individual known to locals as Crazy Larry. If all this isn't enough, add in stories concerning a killer who roams the roads and now shows up in a phantom car that disappears when it approaches you (but you can see the headlights) and ghost lights that are seen bobbing in the direction of the tombstones. This is quite a popular place for the teens to do a little bit of dare action, so be cautious in the area and be respectful of the cemetery and private property.

## I-10 Bridge—Gautier, Mississippi

While the creature in this listing isn't particularly frightening, it certainly makes for an interesting tale. The Pascagoula River has been known for centuries as the Singing River due to a bizarre, musical sound that seems to emanate from the water. It's been estimated that the sounds have been heard as far back as 1699 when French settlers inhabited the area. There are some strange theories involving the source of the singing—including fish, seasonal insects, and even ghosts of the Pascagoula Native American tribe (imagine that)—but the story that raises the most eyebrows is that of the mermaid.

Apparently, the Native Americans in this region believed a mermaid populated the waters and even erected an idol to her. They said she would sing to them when she felt like blessing them with her presence, and they would sing back. When Hernando de Soto arrived, it's said his missionaries saw the mermaid during one of the ceremonies held by the tribe. Today, this bridge makes a good landmark for finding a spot along the Pascagoula to hear the mermaid for yourself. Locals say you have to ask for the singing to hear it; and, of course, the mermaid has to bless you with her presence.

## Enoch Knob Bridge—Franklin County, Missouri

This through truss bridge over Boeuf Creek was recently replaced with a new version, and it's unclear if the old span was destroyed, is awaiting demolition, or is still standing nearby. It doesn't really matter, since the stories involving this spot have a lot to do with the creek and surrounding area—and will most likely carry over to the new bridge.

The most common tale whispered by the locals involve a black demon dog that has been seen stalking the area. Some say you can see its approach because of glowing red eyes (others say the eyes are green). It's a frightening beast either way, say witnesses. But the stories don't stop there. Documented deaths on the bridge have also, seemingly, fueled ghost stories about the span. An accidental death in 1987 and a homicide in 2005 are both public record, so there are incidents that could have resulted in a spirit being left behind at this spot.

Locals have heard disembodied voices on the structure, experienced the failure of electronic devices (including entire vehicles shutting down unexpectedly), and on one occasion, even seen an apparition. For those who enjoy legend tripping, this may be an ideal spot; the reports and activity seem to be of an interesting variety. But it should be noted that people tend to get frightened at this location. Whether it's the vibe in the air or the history of the actual deaths, most do not forget a trip to Boeuf Creek.

## Highway 130 Bridge—Westville, New Jersey

The legend associated with this bridge is often lumped in with the general spookiness of the adjoining River Road. Big Timber Creek was a sacred spot for the Lenape, a Native American tribe that once inhabited the area. It's said that the mysterious mermaid that visits the area surrounding the bridge is an extension of that tribe's folklore.

Sightings of the mermaid are sporadic—and some claim that people still put tributes to it at the site. Otherwise, not much is said or known about this particular phenomenon. Around the corner, though, River Road is known for a female ghost that's said to appear quite regularly. Witnesses say she floats along the road, quite high above the ground, and seems to be wearing either a long dress or a nightgown of some sort. The origins of the spirit are not known, but the two of these stories paired together make for an interesting walking tour.

Take a stroll through downtown Westville and be sure to visit some of the local amenities. After all, how often do you get to visit two paranormal sites that are in close proximity to diners, pubs, and even a bowling alley.

## Tar River Bridge—Pitt County, North Carolina

The old bridge that was located at this spot was recently demolished and replaced with a new concrete span. Don't worry, though, the legend here involves more of the area than it does the bridge itself. What legend? How about "The Legend of the Tar River Banshee"!

It's an old folktale that tells of a Revolutionary War hero named David Warner. David was a miller who supported the patriots and was discovered by the British to be a sympathizer. He was tied to a large stone and tossed into the Tar River, but not before he cursed his killers to be plagued with a banshee. The redcoats' commander, ashamed at the actions of his miscreant troops, ordered the murderers to man the mill as punishment. And they did so until the banshee appeared and took care of them in short order.

Today, the bridge is in the middle of all this spooky action. They say if you hang out on the banks of the river and listen during a moonless night, you will hear the wail of the banshee as it still stalks the area. Sightings of the banshee happen along the river all the way into Edgecombe County. On a side note, there is also a lesser-known ghost story about the bridge. Apparently a young man was accidentally killed by his friends during some horseplay on the span, and now his spirit roams here, too.

## SE 119th Street Bridge—Oklahoma City, Oklahoma

There are a couple scary things about this bridge—one definitely a creature; one not so much. Located across a small tributary running from Kitchen Lake, this bridge and the entire surrounding area host a lot of legendary stories. The most well known, and the source for most legend tripping, is the "Witch of Kitchen Lake."

The remains of a burned home are nearby and is said to be where the witch lived until it caught fire, killing her and destroying the house. These days the evil spirit of the witch is said to roam, causing mischief and burning things at her whim. She also likes to mess with people on the old bridge; vehicles are said to stall indefinitely while crossing, people see rocks flying through the air, and assorted burnt items are often heaped beside the span. In addition to this, sightings of a bigfoot-type monster occur here, too. Some eyewitness accounts describe the thing pretty much like a standard Sasquatch, but some descriptions lean more toward a bearlike thing that gets angry if anyone comes near it.

If this isn't enough for you to take a drive across this bridge, also consider that sightings of spook lights and eerie mists take place here. It's a ghost hunter's dream spot.

## Sheard's Mill Covered Bridge
## —Haycock Township, Pennsylvania

Located along Covered Bridge Road, this circa 1873 covered bridge crosses Tohickon Creek. Folklore historians know it, along with most of the surrounding area, for stories concerning a race of almost-human albinos that roam the region. These demi-humans are known to terrorize those who venture onto Haycock Mountain (known locally as Ghost Mountain), as well as be superstitious themselves. They avoid places on the mountain that they find frightening—such as haunted bridges.

The story goes that if you drive through the bridge, then turn around so that you face it from the other side, and then turn off your car and turn on your lights, you will see what looks like a man hanging inside the bridge. This ghost is also known for appearing on the road as a black mass/figure floating along. This is enough to keep the bridge free of harassment from the albino things—but not enough to keep the ghost hunters away. Interestingly, some say the demi-humans roaming the hills are cannibals.

## Joppa Bridge—Burnet County, Texas

Researchers usually operate in a very structured manner: You observe, gather evidence, and then conjecture based upon that evidence. If you're lucky, your theory will hold up to testing and eventually be proven as fact. The case of the Joppa Trolls is nothing like this. In fact, nobody seems to know anything about the origin story of the supposed creatures inhabiting this area.

The creatures are said to be cowering beneath this historic bridge (it dates back to the early 1900s). Locals say that, if you cross this bridge at certain times, you will hear the noises of trolls beneath. What kinds of noises? Grunting, heavy panting, and the sounds of them scurrying away. Why trolls? Why couldn't this be some sort of animal? Who knows? Trolls!

Since the bridge was replaced with a new version for vehicular traffic, this span is now for pedestrians only. This, of course, is good news for any would-be troll hunter who wants to stake out the area for the monsters.

## Old Alton Bridge—Denton, Texas

If this story hasn't been made into a horror movie of some sort then there are a lot of Hollywood producers who are missing out on a good story. With just enough fact/history mixed with a healthy dose of legend, this may be one of the best spooky bridge tales in all of America.

Constructed in 1884 for the now defunct community of Alton, this old span over Hickory Creek is no longer open to vehicular traffic; a new bridge was built nearby, so this one is now used for pedestrians and equestrians who are using the Elm Fork and Pilot Knoll Trails. This is good news since it means getting there and checking it out is no problem.

The sinister side of this location begins in 1938. A local African-American farmer by the name of Oscar Washburn became well known in the area for his success—and his goats. When the Ku Klux Klan got word of this, they dragged Washburn to the bridge and hung him. However, when they peered below the bridge, the noose was empty. Not knowing if he was alive or dead, they rushed back to his farm and killed the members of his family. Oscar was never seen again (and was presumed dead).

Flash forward thirty years. It's the 1960s and people are seemingly going missing in the area of the bridge. At least three abandoned vehicles and multiple missing person reports indicates something is afoot. Then sightings of a satyr begin. What's a satyr? Essentially, it's a Goat Man. This bizarre spirit/creature has been seen on the bridge and along the creek many times. Add in a mixture of additional scary activity—phantom footsteps/carriage sounds on the bridge, moans and screams in the surrounding woods, and rumors of Satanic rituals—and you have one frightening bridge.

## Pecan Creek Bridge—Hamilton, Texas

It was a toss-up whether this particular bridge should be listed in this chapter or the section about unaccounted oddities. Here's why…

Locals claim that if you take a hike along the Pecan Creek Trail (you can drop into the trail in the Pecan Creek Park) you will eventually come to a bridge that crosses Pecan Creek. Go to the bridge and take a look around; there should be a large, metal drainage pipe nearby. But you may not want to get too close to that pipe. There's supposed to be some sort of creature that lives inside it.

I don't recommend actually doing this, but word on the street is that if you crawl inside a short ways you will see the thing inside peering at you. Some say it is a feral human who found his way into town; some say it is some sort of Goat Man (what is it with Texas and goat men?). Take a buddy along to check out this place—it might be safer that way.

## Donkey Lady Bridge—San Antonio, Texas

In a state full of odd tales about their bridges, it should come as no surprise that one would be known for a terrifying Donkey Lady. This bridge over the Medina River, as well as the neighboring nature park, is said to be the stomping grounds of this bizarre, well, I suppose *creature* is as good a name as any for what she is.

Ask locals about the thing and you'll get this story: A man and his son were camping when they heard some frightening noises coming from the woods. They decided to pack up and leave and had just loaded the car when the Donkey Lady emerged from the trees and leaped on their vehicle. The man took a shot at her then drove to the closest police station to make a report. Sightings of the lady have continued ever since.

So what is this thing? Well, here's another story ... Most say she was a normal person until her home burned down. The fire killed all of her family and horribly burned her, giving her the terrifying look she has today. After that event, years of wandering and mourning in the woods have driven her insane. Now she attacks anyone she sees, hoping to maintain her solitary existence.

## Woman Hollering Creek Bridge—Schertz, Texas

This bridge/creek, like many others in the American southwest, is one of the hangouts of the infamous La Llorona. But here the legend exists with a twist. In most cases, La Llorona is the spirit of a woman who is searching for her dead child; she is known to appear to small children by the water and to approach them, wailing because she is mistaking them for her own. At this bridge, though, the hollering woman is thought to be a succubus—a female demon that sucks the life out of men via sex.

For several decades, people have claimed that the apparition of the wailing woman has wandered the creek and will even attack men who are near the water. So far there haven't been any reports of any ghostly rapes perpetrated against men—but, hey, you never know what can happen these days.

Rather than trying to catch a glimpse of the spirit on the bridge, find a spot along the creek and keep your eyes open. Oh, and the actual name of the place is Woman Hollering Creek by the way. That's not a local nickname.

## Wellington Lane Bridge—Wichita Falls, Texas

What's better than having a state with a Goat Man legend? How about a state that has two bridges with a Goat Man legend! Yes, it's true. Unlike the previous bridge in Denton that has a lot of details and historical notes, this spot is pretty much your basic urban legend fare.

This tiny span on Wellington Lane is supposed to be the lair of a Goat Man who lives underneath it. Apparently a cult/Satanic group was running rampant in the area in the 1970s, and they would use this spot as a dumping ground for sacrificial bodies (mostly animals according to the story). This spawned the demonic thing that now harasses anyone who stops at the bridge. Those brave enough to test the tale have heard growls/cries, seen glowing eyes in the darkness, and even spied the horrible beast itself.

This location is quite popular with local high school students, so the scariest thing you may see if you visit this site is a bunch of underage kids partying and hanging out.

## Long Bridge—Newport, Vermont

There are actually three bridges in the city of Newport that cross the south bay of Lake Memphremagog. Any of them would probably be fine for the purposes of this listing, but the Long Bridge is the most historic of the three (and is due for some renovations soon).

The best spot to do your monster and ghost hunting would probably be on the shore of the lake. Though it is rarely seen close to the city, the entirety of the lake (and it's a big lake that covers some 687 square miles, stretching as far as Magog, Canada) is the hunting ground for a lake monster that's been dubbed Memphre. It has been described to look pretty much like the infamous, and fake, Loch Ness Monster photo with a long neck and almost brontosaurus-like build.

I don't have to tell you that, with a body of water this huge, your chances of catching a glimpse of the creature are pretty slim. You probably have slightly better odds of seeing one of the two other, better-known, regional lake monsters (Champ and Ogopogo). But while you're here, you might want to take a look around for a ghost that's said to hang out, too. It's been claimed that the ghost of Revolutionary War hero General Anthony Wayne also likes to hang out by the lake.

## Silver Memorial Bridge—Point Pleasant, West Virginia

Growing up, one of the earliest memories I have of reading about scary places involves the infamous Mothman and the collapse of the Silver Bridge. On December 15, 1967, the massive bridge collapsed during rush hour traffic, killing forty-six people. It was a horrific tragedy that became a national oddity when writer John Keel unleashed the mystery of the Mothman upon the world.

Said to fall somewhere between space alien, monster, and demon, the Mothman has been seen by numerous locals and has been cited as the cause for quite a few paranormal events in the town of Point Pleasant (including possibly predicting the collapse of the bridge). In the years since the 1960s, there have continued to be sporadic sightings of the Mothman—usually along the water beneath the new bridge or in the surrounding countryside. In addition to this, the bridge has also been the site for a few ghost visitations, too. It seems that some of the souls who drowned in the frigid Ohio River still linger here.

It's a sad story with a healthy dose of the paranormal. There's lots of interesting reading and viewing concerning the Mothman (a movie was made with Richard Gere called *The Mothman Prophecies*) so give it all a look before you head over to this site.

## Shoshone River Bridge—Cedar Mountain, Wyoming

Known also as Spirit Mountain, this spot was a sacred location for the local Native Americans. Standing at 7,890 feet next to a sister mountain, the peak is known for its awesome trails, wonderful views, and the breathtaking Spirit Mountain Cave. It's a great spot for someone to visit to enjoy the great outdoors. But don't be surprised if you notice something else enjoying nature with you—someone about eighteen inches tall.

Much like other tribes in the area, the existence of "little people" was an accepted fact back in the day. Sometimes dubbed *dwarves* by those who have seen them, stories about the little people vary between frightening and mundane. Many of these sightings have taken place along the Shoshone River between the two mountains, so this bridge makes an excellent landmark to begin your adventure. Should you choose to look for these things that is. Lewis and Clark, the famed explorers of the early 1800s, made reference to the little people. They called them little devils and said they would fight anyone who invaded their area using spears/pointy sticks. Sound fun?

## Chapter Eight
# SCENE OF THE CRIME

While we like to think that most of the frightening tales concerning bridges involve the supernatural, the reality is that a lot of horrible, real-world events occurred as well. It's an uncomfortable fact that many of the ghost stories about these structures are rooted in actual murders, lynchings, and worse. Because of this, a healthy dose of respect needs to be in order when exploring the legends detailed in this chapter.

While the spooky spirit of a girl roaming a back road is appealing to us, there may be family members of the poor individual who was killed still in the area. So, by all means, check out the locations listed here—just know that a real person, just like you, perhaps died in the worst of ways at these sites. And be kind to these lost souls.

## Camax Mill Bridge—Jasper, Alabama

Located on Country Club Road, just north of the city, Camax Mill Bridge stands over Black Water Creek. For as long as anyone can remember, people have been sneaking down to the old bridge at night to catch a glimpse of the spirit of Moon Mullins. Though the name actually belongs to an old comic strip character, everyone in Jasper refers to the ghost by this name.

According to the legend, Moon was killed and dumped in the creek beneath the bridge for unknown reasons—and now he walks there each night. Those who have witnessed the activity here report seeing the man's apparition (sometimes on the bridge, oftentimes along the bank of the creek) or see what looks like a massive shadow of a person walking. Visitors have also heard a voice speaking and the sounds of footsteps here.

Interestingly, about the same time that the reputed murder of Mullins took place, a rather unusual photograph of a spirit was taken in Jasper, Alabama, of what looks like a female spirit in a tree. Could the two stories be related in some way?

## Bayview Bridge—Mulga, Alabama

The original bridge at this location was replaced in 1977, but that hasn't stopped a ghost that's been in the area since the 1940s from still appearing. As the story goes, a young woman had just purchased a wedding dress and was on her way home when tragedy struck on the bridge. Most say it was a car accident, but some say she was actually walking when she was attacked by a pack of wild dogs. Either way, she perished and is now doomed to walk the area at night.

Other variations of this haunting include the woman actually fleeing her wedding and her flinging herself off the bridge to escape her betrothed. And, perhaps, the most sinister version of the tale is that the young lady was taking her wedding dress home when she was assaulted, murdered, and then thrown off the bridge into the water below. Whichever version of the story you believe, witnesses of the apparition report that they see her in a long, white dress walking across the bridge. People standing at the lake below have even seen her. Other activity here includes handprints left behind on cars parked on the bridge and mysterious cries in the night.

## Salem-Shotwell Covered Bridge—Opelika, Alabama

Also known as the Pea Ridge Covered Bridge, this structure dates back to 1900. However, due to a massive storm that struck the area in 2005, the bridge was destroyed at its original location close to Salem. The bridge was rebuilt, however, and placed in the Opelika Municipal Park. All of the ghost stories (as well as the incidents that may have created the ghosts) happened at the original location, but locals claim activity is still strong at the new site despite the move.

Interestingly, there are several bizarre stories that are associated with this bridge. The one that is generally agreed upon as the most authentic involves a woman who was found strangled on the bridge (most say this happened in the 1960s). Many have claimed to have seen and heard the spirit of this unfortunate woman. In addition to this ghost story, local urban legends suggest that there was a second woman who perished at the location because of a car accident. Finally, Native Americans were, reportedly, often buried where the structure originally stood—and if you cross this bridge at the right time, their spirits will reach up from the waters to grab you.

## Jones Park Bridge—Arizona City, Arizona

Also known as Happy Days Park, the bridge in question is said to be haunted by a trio of dark entities that reside beneath the structure. The cause of the haunting (according to locals and paranormal investigators) is said to be the rape and death of a young girl that occurred on the site. It's thought that the act was so malevolent that it opened the way for the evil spirits to enter our world.

At any rate, the bridge has had its fair share of paranormal experiences—including people seeing the shadowy spirit of a female and hearing the young girl's death screams. So prevalent are the tales of this bridge that one ghost-hunting group has claimed to have even photographed multiple shadow people under the bridge. Others have claimed to also hear and see things in adjacent areas, including a local playground, the Happy Days RV Park, and even Toltec Elementary School.

## Mill Creek Bridge—Bakersfield, California

This bridge, which spans a small creek in the middle of Bakersfield Central Park, is the site of an eerie spirit that's said to be seen weeping. The bridge was built in 2009 to replace an old wooden structure that was constructed shortly after the park was created in 1921. And, much like the park, locals place the ghost to approximately the same time period.

People who have seen the apparition say she appears in a white dress, and she seems to wander the area around the bridge. She almost always appears close to dawn, and, more often than not, she is seen crying. Local legend says she was murdered across the street from the park in a building that once was the Pacific Southern Foundry. Her bones were apparently discovered as the place was being demolished.

In another version of the story, the young lady was murdered as she strolled through the park, and her body was found facedown in the canal. Either way, there are numerous sightings of this lost spirit, but you better be prepared to get up really early in the morning if you want to catch a glimpse of this haunting.

## Griffin Road Bridge—Wauchula, Florida

Known to locals as Bloody Bucket Bridge, this site is one of the largest tourist attractions in the area. Yes, the story is that well known! According to legend, a midwife who lived in the area (a woman who was once a slave) was known for disposing of unwanted babies. She would smother them and then throw them into the waters below the bridge. After it became obvious that quite a lot of infants were dying/going missing in her care, people stopped using the woman for her services. Of course, at this time, the vengeful spirits of the dead began plaguing her, too…

It's said she began finding a bucket in her home that filled with blood each night. And every night she would take the same bucket to the bridge, and pour the blood into the river there. It was during one of these trips that the woman mysteriously fell into the water and drowned. Some say it was from exhaustion—it's tiring carrying buckets of blood to the river—and some say the angry spirits pushed her.

Since her death, many have claimed to hear the cries of the murdered infants at this location. It's also reported that a visit to the bridge at midnight, when the moon is full, will reveal a river that's red with the blood of the dead.

## Muckalee Creek Bridge—Americus, Georgia

Locals have been telling the story of the ghost girl on Three Bridges Road for many years. And visiting the bridge during the night is a popular rite of passage. If you ask residents in nearby Americus about the spirit you are likely to get one of two tales. The first involves a young girl who was unwanted by her mother and subsequently thrown over the side of the bridge to her death. This is said to have happened sometime in the 1800s.

The second version of the story is even more sinister. Rather than the killer being the girl's mother, the second story states that the girl was abducted, taken to a nearby house, viciously murdered, and then dumped into the creek. Either way, ghost hunters have been drawn to this location for some time.

Ghostly phenomena at this location include the sounds of a girl laughing/crying and the glowing apparition of her floating across the bridge. And, conveniently enough, you will know if the entity is coming if you begin to hear the sounds of a stick banging the rails of the span as she slowly walks across it…

If you decide to check this one out, make sure the bridge is on public property; there is conflicting information regarding ownership of the bridge and the surrounding land.

## Alcovy Trestle Bridge—Covington, Georgia

It's best to begin this listing with a warning. Train trestles—especially those with no walkways and active trains crossing them—are dangerous places. So do not attempt to walk out on one! That said, the sightings of ghosts at this location were safely made from nearby. And, yes, there's more than one spirit.

The first apparition seen on the tracks seems to be a young African-American woman who sometimes glows as she walks along. It's said vigilantes hung her from the bridge in the 1940s for messing around with a local white boy. Though this story cannot be verified for authenticity, it is widely known throughout the area.

The second ghost at this bridge, however, is said to be the product of a well-documented crime that took place in the 1980s. A young boy was playing at a local arcade when a known criminal offered him a ride home. The boy and his bike were loaded in a pickup—and, unfortunately, he never made it home. The small body was found in a clearing near the trestle. Witnesses to the boy's spirit say he appears riding his bike and that he pays no attention to those around him. He seems to be in a hurry, perhaps trying to outrun the horrible tragedy that was his death.

## Parrish Mill Covered Bridge —Emanuel County, Georgia

Located within George L. Smith State Park, this covered bridge dates back to 1880 and is part of a unique getaway. It's located alongside a mill, a pond, and a dam and is quite the local tourist attraction. As for the ghost story—well, this one may be a little bit difficult to experience…

Apparently, if you drive your car barely onto the bridge, turn it off, exit the vehicle, and place the keys on the hood, you will have a strange encounter. You're supposed to walk to the other end of the bridge and turn around; at that point you will notice that your car is now running without you and a mysterious light is glowing on the pond. The reason for this supposed occurrence is that a man drove to this exact spot in the 1930s, where he then murdered his wife in the waters below. This is all a dramatic recreation of these events.

But, as I mentioned, it will be rather difficult to test whether this actually works or not, since this particular bridge is now pedestrian only and closed to vehicular traffic. I'm sure some of you who are reading this have creative minds. See if you can get the spirit on the water to appear by other means.

## Withlacoochee River Bridge—Valdosta, Georgia

With a nickname like Spook Bridge, this spot is sure to be haunted. The actual name of this span between Brooks and Lowndes

County is Withlacoochee River Bridge, and it's only accessible by a lengthy hike. Once you get there, well, you may want to look at the bridge from afar since it is quite dilapidated and dangerous to actually tread upon. With a reputation that's known statewide, this area is quite popular with thrill seekers, ghost hunters, and those who are simply curious about the story behind this spot.

It seems that a married couple lived nearby, and after a furious fight one evening, the husband killed the wife. Some say this happened in the home, some say it happened on the bridge. Either way, people now claim to see the spirit of the woman climbing from the water onto the bridge. But you don't earn a moniker like Spook Bridge with just one story. Additional tales about this place include a bus that drove off the bridge (killing all the kids inside), satanic rituals that were held nearby, and a murder that happened in 1999 (true story).

It all adds up to a terrifying visit—just make sure you're safe making the trek. You may want to check in with one of the local sheriff's offices (depending on which county you approach from) since the bridge also has a reputation for illegal activities.

## Lower Loon Creek Bridge
## —Salmon-Challis National Forest, Idaho

If you make your way to this stellar state park located just outside Boise, you will want to check your trail map for Loon Creek Trail #4104. The beginning of this trail is the Lower Loon Creek Bridge—and this landmark is the start of a twenty-mile hike that takes you right through haunted country.

Legend states that a man by the name of Manuel Sato was camping in this area in 1870 when a group of highwaymen fell upon him. The men were escaping from another heist (a local bank robbery) when they decided to rob and kill Sato. When a posse set out to find the killers, they found Sato's old campsite and a bit more. The ghostly visage of old Sato was seen there, leading along a set of ethereal pack mules.

The country surrounding this area and along the trail is beautiful and remote; cellphone service is scarce, wildlife is in abundance, and the trail is very long. So if you plan to make the hike, prepare in advance and you will be rewarded with a gorgeous journey through Idaho.

## Airtight Bridge—Coles County, Illinois

Built in 1914 by the Decatur Bridge Company, this truss bridge over the Embarras River was the scene of a horrific murder. On October 19, 1980, a pair of deer hunters were driving along Airtight Road when they noticed a naked body floating in the water beneath the bridge. After a quick investigation, they discovered a female dismembered corpse. The killer had removed the head, hands, and feet from the body. Because of this, the Torso Murder would be a difficult one for local law enforcement to tackle. It would be November 20, 1992, before DNA testing would reveal the identity of the murdered girl—but, unfortunately, the killing remains unsolved today.

Of course, with an incident like this occurring at this location, it comes as no surprise that the place is considered haunted. People who visit the bridge say there's an unnatural stillness in the air, and it doesn't take long to feel a bizarre presence while crossing the bridge. Local ghost hunters have performed investigations under the structure and have claimed to hear voices/cries, see a misty figure on the riverbank, and to even be touched by an unseen hand. Sometimes history and a haunting collide—these stories carry a lot of impact because of the associated truth with them. So be respectful when visiting these locations.

## Old Post Road Bridge—Crete, Illinois

This simple concrete bridge crossing over Plum Creek looks anything but scary. But if you stop nearby and take a look just up the creek, you will notice the remains of an older bridge that's now covered with graffiti and rust. It's said the broken bridge is the site of a horrific crime—though the exact details of the crime are debated locally.

The old bridge, as well as the remains of a nearby house, is associated with a person known as the Axe Man. He is called this because of a series of murders he performed using, well, an ax. In one version of the story, Axe Man killed a pair of kids who were doing dares on the bridge. In another, he slaughtered his own family and a couple local police officers who were investigating the incident.

Whichever you believe, in the aftermath of all this violence, many claim that the area is haunted. Cars are known to fail on the Old Post Road Bridge, people have seen ghostly lights in the woods (supposedly the light shining through the windows from the Axe Man's old home), and heard the sounds of the dead screaming in the night. If all of this isn't scary enough for you, also consider that people have also heard the sounds of an ax chopping in the woods, as well as heard the phantom footsteps of the Axe Man walking across the bridge…headed straight for those who stop there.

## Lakey's Creek Bridge—McLeansboro, Illinois

Sometimes a story is so good that is doesn't matter whether it's truth or fiction. Such is the case with the bizarre tale of an old settler named Lakey. He was building a nice little cabin alongside the creek that's now named for him, when a neighbor came over for a visit. The two chatted for a while before parting ways. And that was the last that anyone saw of old Lakey until his decapitated body was found nearby. A few days after the funeral of the old man (he was buried by his partially built cabin), a couple was traveling along when they saw a headless man appear on a black stallion. The pair fled in fear.

Years later, a bridge was built over the creek, and the ghost of Lakey continued to appear. Now, more than a hundred years later, people continue to see the headless ghost on a horse. It's said that if you approach the bridge from the east, your chances of seeing the apparition increase considerably. Many surmise that this was the direction the killer approached old Lakey from—and now his spirit rises in the hopes of finding justice.

Though the story sounds like a good urban legend, dozens of people have claimed to have seen the headless spirit. And, though his visage is said to be frightening, the ghost always disappears shortly after being seen.

## Norris Ford Covered Bridge—Rush County, Indiana

Located on County Road 300 (CR300), this circa 1916 structure spans the Flatrock River. Being one of five covered bridges in this county, it is quite a tourist attraction in the area. Of course, not everyone goes there for the lovely architecture ...

The ghost who haunts this bridge has been whispered about for generations—and for locals, parking inside this bridge at midnight is a rite of passage for teenagers who have just gotten their driver's licenses. So, who haunts this spot? The short, and boring, version of the background story says the spirit is a young woman who perished in an auto accident. She is said to have driven into the river and drowned there, along with her child.

The better version of the story also says the ghost is a young woman, but states the woman died after falling from the bridge's rafters. It seems the townsfolk believed the woman to be a witch; she didn't go to church, she had a child out of wedlock, and she was seen buying herbs. So she had to be a witch, right? When her baby was born, an angry mob descended upon her home and found her with the dead child. The woman fled and hid in the bridge. After she was spotted hiding there, the townsfolk prodded at her until she fell to her demise. The baby had perished of natural causes, but the young woman left the world an angry spirit. Now she bangs on the cars of frightened teenagers.

## Rocky Ford Bridge—Emporia, Kansas

When the body of a young woman was found in her car that had washed beneath the bridge in the Cottonwood River, it was initially ruled death by accident. It was July 17, 1983, and local law enforcement was anything but prepared to deal with what would turn out to be a murder (double murder in the end). It would be after a second body was found that the pieces of a horrible puzzle would fall into place. The first victim's husband, a local minister, was having an affair with a lady who lived in the area. At some point the two of them decided to do away with their spouses, with the aid of a couple local thugs. All involved were arrested and convicted in the end, and that would have been the end of the story if not for spooky happenings at the old bridge…

Since the death of the woman, people have seen her spirit wandering the area beside the river—and on occasion, the sounds of her death screams piercing the night. With so much of this story falling into the realm of fact, this haunted bridge seems particularly compelling. It also helps that the affair and murder were detailed in a movie titled *Murder Ordained*. Maybe you want to check it out before you spend a night looking for the lonely soul who wanders this structure.

## Carter Bridge—Oak Grove, Kentucky

While most hauntings stir up a fair amount of debate (*Is there really a ghost? Did anyone actually die at this location?*), this bridge has particularly been a hotbed of discussion among paranormal groups in Kentucky. There are those who have investigated the area and claim to have gotten evidence of the activity, and there are those who have spent a lot of time debunking the legends associated with this location.

Locals claim a female spirit, who often appears in various states of decay, haunts the bridge. She usually appears on the bridge, but sometimes below. She's said to have been murdered by her significant other, a soldier at nearby Fort Campbell. Attempts to verify this crime have all been fruitless. There was, however, a crime quite similar to this that happened in the 1920s in the town of Hopkinsville, so it's entirely possible that people have confused the two locations. The Hopkinsville murder ended with a death sentence that was carried out for the former soldier who had murdered his wife (and hid her body underwater).

Despite the possible confusion, people insist Carter Bridge is haunted. Online details of investigations include cold spots on the bridge, ghostly voices, and the visage of the rotting woman staggering along the road.

## Bayou Tortue Road Bridge—Broussard, Louisiana

Known throughout the region as Mary Jane's Bridge, this particular haunting has been covered for years by local newspapers, radio stations, etc., that needed a great place to talk about during the Halloween season. Most people agree that the background story of the bridge is most likely fabricated (probably by parents who wanted to keep their kids out of trouble on prom night), but the tale persists and people still flock to this location to catch a glimpse of the Lady in White. So who is this mysterious woman?

The story goes that a young couple was at the prom when they decided to go park at the bridge to get to know one another a little better. When the girl cut the boy off from going a bit too far, he became angry and then raped, killed, and tossed the girl off the bridge. Since that night, the girl wanders this spot—still decked out in her white prom dress.

Many have claimed to have seen this apparition, as well as hear her screams in the night. Purportedly a police officer who lives in the area once spotted the girl and, thinking she was a live human needing help, he approached her, but she was unresponsive to his questions. Then she disappeared. If this isn't enough to get you to visit Mary Jane, also consider that tales of a second spirit are also associated with the structure. The spirit of an ax-wielding killer.

## Marland's Bridge—Sunset, Louisiana

Named after Congressional Medal of Honor recipient William Marland for his heroic deeds during the American Civil War, this bridge is said to be haunted by the apparition of a woman dressed in white. Legend states that she was on her way to a nearby church to get married when she was intercepted, killed, and thrown into Bayou Bourbeau.

Visitors to the span today are occasionally treated to the appearance of the dead bride-to-be—often accompanied by the sounds of her death screams. Interestingly, the spirit is known to mess with people's car radios when they drive across the bridge, too. Maybe this could be a sort of ghost alarm for people brave enough to check out the place at night. If you're approaching the bridge and your radio starts going crazy, maybe you will be getting a visit.

Of course, apparitions aside, the spot is a historic site associated with the Civil War battle called the Battle of Bayou Bourbeau that happened here in 1863. It was during this skirmish that William Marland earned his medal by charging a group of Confederate soldiers with his horse-drawn wagon, thereby saving himself, knocking enemy troops into the bayou, and liberating a piece of artillery from being captured by the enemy.

## Rogue River Bridge—Algoma Township, Michigan

Ask most people in this area of Michigan about a man named Elias Friske and you will get an earful. Almost everyone knows the story—or at least a variation of it. Before the city of Algoma Township existed, the local town was called Rockford. This tale takes place during that period.

It's said that the local parish was meeting in church to discuss a missing child when a search party was formed to look for him/her. The remaining children were left at the church under the care of one Elias Friske. Turns out this was a bad choice of guardian. He promptly guided all the kids to Rogue River and killed them. When everyone returned to the church and found the children gone, they promptly set out after Elias. They found him close to the river, along with their dead offspring, and promptly decided to hang him. Of course, Friske claimed that he was possessed by the devil when he did the horrible deed, but that did not dissuade the parishioners from stringing him up.

Today, there is a nice bridge that crosses the river. It's just up the way from Friske Drive, along a walking trail. It's a great place to go hang out by the river, as long as you don't go at night… The span is known as Hell's Bridge these days and many a person has claimed to have experienced the haunting here. Activity includes the sounds of children screaming, otherworldly moans and groans, and the frightening sight of Elias standing either on the bank or on the bridge.

## Nine Mile Bridge—Auxvasse, Missouri

This bridge located along County Road 156 (CR156) has had a most horrible history associated with it—whether that history is actually true or false. Locals say that in the days preceding the American Civil War, slave holders would use Auxvasse Creek to drown and dispose of African-American slaves that they did not want. Usually these were female children, but on occasion, adults were apparently killed as well. Because of this, a lot of spooky things happen at the spot now dubbed Nine Mile Bridge.

Activity at the location includes sightings of a female apparition wandering the bridge, crying and pleading voices emanating from the area of the water, and even odd footsteps seemingly coming from all around you. In addition to this, there are a couple dares associated with the bridge, too. The first involves parking your car. This may produce phantom handprints on your vehicle—or cause the car to not start, which means you now have to push it off the bridge. The second, more interesting, dare requires you to sit on the edge of the bridge with your shoes off. If you do this, locals say you will feel small hands tickle the bottom of your feet. Whichever you decide to do, please be aware that there is traffic on this road/ bridge.

## Rosemary Road Bridge—Florence, Missouri

A word of warning: This historic bridge is now closed to vehicular traffic and is most likely unfit to even walk upon safely. That said, you can certainly check out the bridge and do some ghost watching from afar.

Unfortunately, there aren't many details available concerning the haunting at this spot. For decades, people living in the area have told the campfire tale of a woman named Rosemary who was murdered on the bridge in the 1950s. It's uncertain if her name was actually Rosemary or if she was dubbed that because of the road. Either way, numerous people in the region surrounding the old bridge have seen her spirit. Most say she seems kind of out of it and that she goes about her way, oblivious of anyone who is watching.

I could find no historical records of a murder at this location, but it does seem that a lot of people have seen this lonely apparition. If you take a trip into Florence to do some ghost hunting, just be careful and don't mess around on the rickety old bridge—and be sure to snap a picture of Rosemary. We need a few more details about this spectral lady.

## Stone Arch Bridge—Kenoza Lake, New York

Built in 1880 by Henry and Philip Hembdt, a couple of Swiss/ German immigrants, this bridge is listed on the National Register of Historic Places. It's known as a local landmark and for a rather historic crime known as the Hex Murder. This was one of the earliest recorded homicides in the area, but ironically would not be the only killing of this type.

The time was 1882 and the victim at this bridge was one George Markert. He was killed by a local farmer named Adam Heidt and his son Joseph because they thought that George had placed a hex upon them. They saw him crossing this old bridge one night and fell upon him with a club and a revolver. His body was dumped into the water below. Joseph went to prison for the crime, while Adam was sent to a mental health facility.

Since that fateful day, people claim to see the misty apparition of George hanging out on the bridge. The entire area here is gorgeous and is worth visiting even without the ghost story. It should be noted that Native Americans in the area held that the lake itself had mystical powers, and they tell a few spooky tales about it, too ...

## Chair Factory Road Bridge
## —Columbus County, North Carolina

Spanning Monie Swamp, this small bridge southeast of the town of Williams is known for a rather interesting anomaly. It's said that if you drive across this bridge at certain times (midnight and sunset seem to be mentioned a lot) you will begin hearing the sound of a heart beating. That sound will get louder and louder until you finally cross the bridge and put the place behind you. This is supposed to be the haunting presence of a girl who was killed on the bridge; her heart was cut out by her murderer and tossed into the swamp below. Now she torments everyone, waiting until the day her killer is brought to justice. That killer has never been found—in fact, there's no proof that there ever was a killer or even a body found at this spot—so the legend of Heartbeat Bridge continues.

This tale is very well known throughout North Carolina, and it has appeared in countless tomes of folktales and legends. Enjoy a drive through the countryside and check out the spot for yourself.

## Greely Chapel Road Bridge—Allen County, Ohio

While the current bridge standing at this spot over the Auglaize River was erected in 2001, the previous incarnation of the structure dated back to 1906. So it has been around (in one form or another) for quite some time. I only say this because the legend associated with this bridge has been around almost as long. Well, it's been around for as long as automobiles have existed anyway …

The story goes that a carload of young folks were out on this stretch of road when tragedy struck. They were all found murdered, their corpses scattered about the area of the bridge. There's some debate as to how many were actually killed, but it seems to be three to six individuals. At any rate, encounters with the remnants of this horrible act, as well as with the ghosts themselves, have been talked about around campfires for decades. Some say they hear the screams and moans of those who were murdered, some say they see ghosts walking along the road, and some say the entire grisly scene sometimes appears. In the latter case, the car the kids were riding in, as well as the bodies, is seen just as it was when the act happened so many years ago.

## Tindall Bridge—Ballville, Ohio

Built in 1915 by the Champion Iron Company over the Sandusky River, this old bridge was the site of a gruesome murder in 1955. A recently released convict by the name of Sam Tannyhill decided to rob a diner in Fremont and ended up taking a hostage by the name of Shirley Bradford. There's conflicting information as to what went wrong, but Tannyhill ended up killing Bradford on the Tindall Bridge and tossing her body into the water below. Her body was found the following day. Tannyhill had fled to Missouri.

He was later caught, convicted of the murder, and was executed for the crime.

Unfortunately, many say that Shirley never left the bridge. Her apparition is seen on and below the structure, and the sounds of her screams as she was bludgeoned to death are heard in the night. Some say her spirit will approach you or your vehicle sobbing for help with her arms out. If that's true, it's one of the saddest ghost stories listed here. This bridge does experience rather heavy traffic, so be careful if you visit. It's located on County Road 209 (CR209) south of town.

## Ridge Avenue Bridge—Dayton, Ohio

Known locally as Bessie Little's Bridge, this structure over the Stillwater River is one of the most well-known haunted spots in all of Ohio—and it's certainly a tourist draw for people visiting Dayton. The apparition of a woman named Bessie Little is said to be seen on the span quite regularly, along with the sounds of her ghostly screams.

This particular story is actually based on a true story. On August 27, 1896, a man named Albert J. Frantz killed Bessie when he discovered that she was pregnant with his child. Frantz attempted to make the crime look like a suicide, but he was arrested and eventually executed in 1897. Now the sad spirit of Bessie walks the bridge over the spot where her body was found.

Finding this spot is not very hard; practically everyone knows the story. But if you doubt that you've found the right bridge, know that there is a plaque mounted nearby that says this structure is named the 134th D Artillery Memorial Bridge (it is named for a unit that fought in World War I known as Battery D, 134th Field

Artillery, 37th Division). But then how are you going to miss a bridge with a ghostly girl standing in the middle of it?

## Bloody Bridge—Spencerville, Ohio

There are so many things to like about this bridge. First of all, how about the fact that it's actually called Bloody Bridge! It's not a nickname. That is its actual name. Another thing that makes this particular spot stand out is the sheer amount of facts that are available to support the haunting here. There is actually a plaque at the site, placed there by the Auglaize County Historical Society, that tells the story behind the bridge best:

"During the canal years of the 1850s, a rivalry grew between Bill Jones and Jack Billings for the love of Minnie Warren. This became hatred by Bill, because Minnie chose Jack. On a fall night in 1854, returning from a party, Minnie and Jack were surprised on the bridge by Bill, armed with an ax. With one swing, Bill severed Jack's head. Seeing this, Minnie screamed and fell from the bridge into a watery grave. Bill disappeared, and when a skeleton was found years later in a nearby well, people asked was it suicide or justice."

So, there you have it. Two dead, one killer. Because of this bloody tale, people have now seen the spirit of Minnie on the bridge, though sometimes it's said she's also seen peering from the depths of the canal. If this isn't enough haunting for you, also consider that a few folks have claimed to see a headless ghost on the bridge, too. See, I told you this bridge is awesome.

## Lee Roy's Bridge—Gaffney, South Carolina

During the years of 1967 and 1968, a serial killer terrorized the residents of Gaffney. When the first victim was found murdered, the town had no idea it even had a serial killer. The victim's husband had been arrested and convicted of the crime. So everyone thought the case was closed. It wasn't until the killer struck again in 1968, and he called the local paper to confess to the first killing, that the manhunt began. Lee Roy Martin was eventually caught and convicted for four murders.

Several of the spots where Martin strangled and raped his victims (in that order) are now considered haunted. This bridge, located just off Highway 329, was the site of the second murder—and the ghost of the young girl who was killed is said to still be present. Witnesses say the tormented spirit has been spotted by the creek under the bridge, and her disembodied voice has been heard pleading for help. It's a horrible true story with a sad, haunted ending. Be respectful when checking out this site. The town of Gaffney still remembers those horrible days in 1968.

## Three Bridges Road—Powdersville, South Carolina

This is another one of those stories that could go in several chapters of this book. It's historical, it's sad, and it concerns the killing of a slave girl named Eloise. The story goes that Union soldiers stormed a neighboring plantation toward the end of the American Civil War. They killed the landowner, but spared the young slave girl. At least they spared her until she began mourning for the man who was now dead. Angry at her lack of appreciation for her newfound liberation, the soldiers went ahead and killed her, too.

Today, the plantation is long gone, but the sad spirit of Eloise still roams the road that now crosses her old farm. While there may be multiple bridges on this road (hey, it's called Three Bridges Road for a reason), you will probably want to do your ghost watching in the vicinity of the span over Middle Branch Brushy Creek. This seems to be the hotspot for Eloise sightings. Good luck!

## Watauga River Bridge—Elizabethton, Tennessee

The story about this haunting first appeared in the book *Haints, Witches, and Boogers: Tales From Upper East Tennessee.* The name of the book is so awesome I just had to mention it! This ghost story concerns the double homicide of Tom Jackson and Wanda Smithson. The two were courting at this bridge when they noticed a man approaching them—a man carrying a knife. Wanda was stabbed and killed there on the spot; Tom was stabbed, but he managed to get to a person in a parked vehicle not far away. They drove away, but he later died of the wounds. Police had the body of Tom, but when they returned to the bridge, the body of Wanda was gone. The murderer was never identified or caught.

Not long after the gruesome attack, people started noticing some odd things on the bridge. There were sounds of people walking when nobody was around and a dark, shadowy figure was often seen there. Most believe the ghost is Tom, riddled with guilt for not saving Wanda. It's said, if you're lucky, some nights you can hear most of the horrible evening reenacted: You will hear footsteps, screams, and what sounds like a car door slamming. It's a weird and sad tale.

## Burnt Mill Bridge—Scott County, Tennessee

Built in 1920, this abandoned bridge stands side by side with the new span that took its place over Clear Fork River (located on Honey Creek Loop Road). This is a great situation for ghost watching; you can pull over on the road before crossing the new bridge and watch this place with a clear, unobstructed view. Maybe then you can see the apparition that's been spotted walking here.

Locals say a young girl was murdered here in the 1960s—some indicate her father did it, some believe it was a killer at large. She was killed and thrown over the side. Now her sad spirit roams the bridge and, on some nights, can be seen falling from the structure.

While I did not find any supporting facts for a murder at this spot in the 1960s, I did find an eyewitness account concerning the ghost. This person said he saw a young girl dressed in white standing on the bridge, staring into the water below. Then she fell off, as if dead, and hit the river without a splash. Might be worth going there for a look-see.

## Moeller Road Bridge—Electra, Texas

There are tales of three murders told about this particular bridge—all of them may be completely untrue. But that hasn't stopped stories about ghosts from circulating the area. Known as Screaming Sheila Bridge for miles around, this dilapidated span over China Creek is a mess. Seriously. Don't even think about trying to cross it in any fashion. Visit it if you like, but do your ghost watching from afar.

As mentioned, there are three possible women who may have been killed at this site. The first was a witch who was reputedly burned on the bridge in the 1800s for practicing her craft. The second was a victim of a car crash who burned inside the vehicle; this is still referred to as a murder of sorts since she had been in an argument with her husband prior to the wreck and he intentionally left her in the car to die. The third possible victim was a woman who had been caught cheating on her husband. He talked her into going to the bridge with him where she was waylaid by friends of the man. They beat her there till she was dead and burned her body. The common denominators here: A woman was killed and her name was Sheila. And if you visit this bridge in the wee hours, her screams are said to echo throughout the area.

## Broadway Avenue Bridge—Haltom City, Texas

While I could not verify the story about the murder at this bridge, residents of Haltom City swear it's true. In the 1990s, a young boy turned up missing from a school nearby. A few days went by without him showing back up, until a couple other students found the body beside Big Fossil Creek. The murderer was never found, but the spirit of the boy still roams the area. He's been seen along the creek under the bridge and in neighboring Barbrook Park.

Witnesses to the activity say you can hear heavy breathing, moaning, and cries around the bridge; however, his full-blown apparition can be seen walking through the trees of the park and woods. It has been surmised that, perhaps, he was killed in the park and his body was dumped in the creek. But as I said before, I couldn't verify there was a murder at all. Do some investigating and maybe you can turn up more information regarding this case and haunting.

## Old Buffalo Lake Bridge—Iowa Park, Texas

This old wooden bridge close to Burnett Park burned down years ago, but the remains are still present—and that's pretty much all you will need if you decide to check out this haunted spot. You will want to find a good location to park at the lake and then walk to the area with the bridge. Once you are there, locals say a creepy feeling will come over you; then you will hear a woman start screaming.

But don't run yet. The female apparition just might appear and run up to you, still screaming of course.

The story behind this activity is that a woman was attacked in her car at the bridge; she was raped and murdered by two men, who were later trapped nearby and killed by police officers. Others say the screams are victims of a cult that plagues the area and add that a black figure has been seen at the lake, too. Either way, just know that this area has been a bad spot for crimes; a body was found buried at the park as recently as 2012 and several rapes/assaults have been documented here. So be sure to take a ghost-hunting buddy along with you if you're checking out this site.

## Old Leakey Road Bridge—Rio Frio, Texas

The winding river that weaves around the town of Rio Frio is known by several names; in fact, it changes names on the map several times. At one point it is called Pailing Creek, then it changes to Cherry Creek, and further south it becomes the Frio River. The ghostly legend is associated with the Frio River, but the bridge listed here is right in the middle of the haunted action that seems to happen up and down this stretch of water.

The activity surrounds the ghost of a young girl named Maria, who is better known locally as the White Lady. Maria is said to have been killed by a jealous brother-in-law when she spurned his advances. This story dates back to the early 1900s, so that's a long time for people to be talking about the spirit that haunts this area. It's said that the ghost appears as a wispy, ethereal apparition floating along the river. The only thing that is unclear is why Maria has anything to do with the river at all since she was killed with a pistol on a local farm.

If you want to up your chances of catching sight of this ghost, start at the bridge and work your way south along the river; the stretch between the bridge and the Frio River branch is where most sightings take place.

## Dyreson Road Bridge—Dunn, Wisconsin

Dating back to 1897, this historic bridge remains in limbo until the city of Dunn figures out what to do with it. It has been closed to vehicular traffic and is now waiting restoration. Hanging over the Yahara River like an ancient relic, this bridge is one of the last truss bridges in the state, so it's hoped that it will live on. In the meantime, there's a haunting at this bridge concerning someone who did not live on.

The story goes that a black car was speeding along when the driver spied someone walking across the bridge. Rather than slowing down and attempting to avoid the pedestrian, the car ran the woman down. The acts of that evening repeat now and again. People claim to see the phantom car tearing along the road—screaming up behind them as they are driving—until it finally disappears into thin air. Often accompanying this is the sound of a disembodied voice screaming.

There are a few different eyewitness accounts of this activity, though sometimes the person only hears the screams or only sees the car. Take a drive down the rustic Dyreson Road and maybe you'll see the scary black car, too.

## Chapter Nine
# MYSTERIOUS LIGHTS

People have been baffled by spook lights for centuries. Native Americans viewed them as lost spirits that were to be avoided and many cultures believe them to be supernatural creatures—much like the legendary will-'o-the-wisp. Today, attitudes bounce between the mundane (swamp gas, ball lightning, etc.) and the fantastic (ghosts, demons, etc.). Whatever your viewpoint may be, encountering these lights along a lonely set of train tracks, road, or bridge is an event that's not easily forgotten. This chapter is all about those mysterious lights that haunt and fascinate us even today and the stories that attempt to explain them.

## Billy's Bridge—Mena, Arkansas
Tales of Billy's Bridge have been circulating the towns of Potter and Mena for almost a hundred years, so that should give you an idea of the history that involves this location. While the story surrounding the haunting of this site will seem quite familiar, it's the appearance of the spirit itself that stands out.

According to legend, an old horse-drawn wagon was crossing the bridge when a wheel became dislodged, turning the wagon over and tumbling everyone/everything out. When the driver was able to recover, it was found that a young man named Billy had perished. Since then, the ghost of the lad has been seen here regularly.

On most occasions, Billy makes himself known by banging on the bridge or by stomping loudly across the structure. But now and then, Billy seems to appear as a ghost light that glides along the roadway over the bridge. Those who have seen him in this form say the light exhibits intelligence—it will weave and bob around objects and even stop in midair. At least one witness has also claimed that Billy will appear in normal (little boy) form, too. Of course, this person additionally said that the spirit tried to push him off the bridge.

The only difficulty with getting to this location is finding it. Locals will most likely be able to point you in the right direction, but accounts vary on the exact position of the bridge.

## Bellamy Bridge—Marianna, Florida

This location is the site of one of Florida's most well-known ghost stories. Each year thousands of curious visitors venture to this old bridge to see the mysterious balls of fire that are said to shoot across the span. Sometimes the spirit chooses to appear as a female apparition, dressed all in white, or as regular balls of light strolling along the banks of the Chipola River. But who is the entity that haunts this spot?

According to legend, it is Elizabeth Jane Croom Bellamy. It's said that on her wedding day, she accidentally caught her dress on fire. She then panicked and ran into the woods to the river, hoping to put out the flames. After accomplishing this task, though, she was left with severe burns that ended up killing her.

Elizabeth Bellamy's story is known throughout the area—and it does appear that local records support the existence of the girl. But she did not die in a fire. It seems that, in reality, Elizabeth died of natural causes—most likely yellow fever.

So who actually haunts the place? Your guess is as good as mine! Even with an incorrect legend, though, dozens of people have reported seeing the apparition of a young woman on this bridge along with the mysterious lights. If you want to make a trip to see Elizabeth, make sure to take the Bellamy Bridge Heritage Trail to get there. Automobiles no longer drive on the bridge and Bellamy Bridge Road is no longer open to the public.

## Little Econ River Bridge—Orange County, Florida

Talk to people who live in this area and you will get an earful concerning the legendary Oviedo Lights. They are usually spotted on the stretch of road that connects the towns of Oviedo and Chuluota, right around the bridge that crosses the Econlockhatchee River. Most witnesses see a single, green light that seems to dance in the distance, but on rare occasions, multiple lights are also seen. Researchers have attributed the phenomenon to a type of algae that glows, but many believe the lights are associated with another nearby story/bridge...

Tales of Christopher "Killer" Klink have been whispered around campfires in the area for many years. He is associated with a rather unique (and strangely specific) ghost story. It seems if you happen to make your way along the Little Econ River on October 13, and pass under the Little Econ Bridge stationed along Old Econ Road, you will witness the appearance of Killer Klink's apparition. It's said a bright flash of light will occur followed by the appearance of the ghost hanging from the bridge. Legend states that you will know the event is about to happen when the air gets strangely frigid and the flow of the river seems to reverse.

Investigators have made many attempts to find a record of Mr. Klink living or dying in the area and nothing has come to light as of yet. Even more frustrating is a lack of information about Klink on an urban legend level. There seems to be no details as to who Klink was supposed to be, how he came to haunt the bridge, or even what he did to deserve this particular afterlife. But that hasn't stopped people from visiting the bridge every year to see if he appears.

## Hardin Bridge—Bartow County, Georgia

The Austin Brothers Bridge Company built this truss bridge over the Etowah River in 1930, and it functioned until 2007. In 2011, a new span was opened nearby and the original was retired. It was eventually torn down in 2015. But that hasn't stopped the nightly, haunted activity at this location.

If you visit the new bridge, keep an eye out for a pair of mysterious lights that seem to be headed toward the river. They are said to be the headlights of a car long gone. Legend states that a couple was crossing the old wooden bridge when they saw an approaching vehicle. Since it only had room for one-way traffic, the driver panicked and drove over the side of the bridge, plunging them to their deaths.

In addition to the lights, people say the screams of terror made by the couple can be heard in the night. Since this site has been a popular nocturnal attraction since the 1960s, it's assumed the deaths occurred prior to that. And while glowing lights and death screams seem to be a little ... well, scary ... most say the experience is quite tame.

## Highway 341 Bridge—Surrency, Georgia

The stories surrounding this locally famous spook light make for some fascinating reading, but before we get to that it's best to identify the location for seeing this phenomenon. Beneath this bridge is a set of train tracks—and it is here that most people see the bizarre, glowing ball of light floating along.

Like most ghost lights, people have used the typical gamut of explanations for the activity: Swamp gas, ball lightning, reflections from oncoming headlights, etc. But if you ask the locals, you will get one or more of the following interesting tales ...

The first explanation involves an urban legend about a husband and a wife who lived close to the tracks. It's said they had a heated argument one evening that ended with the woman storming out the door, onto the tracks, and into the path of an oncoming train. The ghost light is supposed to be the spirit of the husband eternally looking for her.

The most interesting background story of the spook light, though, involves a well-documented poltergeist haunting that happened in Surrency in 1872. The victims of said ghostly activity were Allen Powel Surrency and his family. According to written reports, the family would suffer dishes flying through the air, unexplained voices and screams, doors opening and closing by themselves, and even farm animals magically appearing in the house. Witnesses to the activity number more than fifty, and it's said the poltergeist haunting continued until Allen's death in 1877. Many believe the ghost light is the mischievous spirit that plagued him in the house—and others say it is Allen himself looking for peace and quiet in the afterlife.

## Coon Creek Bridge—Barnes, Kansas

Sometimes a ghost story doesn't have to be all that compelling to draw a crowd. Ask anyone in the area surrounding Barnes, Kansas, about the ghost at Coon Creek Bridge, and you will hear all about it. Unfortunately, the story will be about how scary the apparition is, or how sorry they feel for the spirit, or how nobody knows who died there. And that's about it, really. Except for the actual ghost.

People say the apparition of a young girl is seen wandering the area around the bridge in the wee hours of the morning—usually the hour or two leading up to sunrise. And if you go there around midnight, you will spy a bright, glowing orb of light that seems to take the same path as the spectral girl. But whether it's a ghost light or a full-blown ghost, no one seems to know who she is, how she got to be where she's at, or how she moved on to the afterlife. But doesn't this make the story all the more compelling? There's no urban legend and no familiar details that seem to mirror a hundred other haunted places. Just the ghost of a girl who walks along a lonely road…

## Jester's Creek Bridge—Valley Center, Kansas

Known throughout the state as Theorosa's Bridge, you could argue that this may be the most visited haunted locale in the territory. Dozens of witnesses have claimed to have seen either ghost lights or a female apparition at this bridge. While most tend to think of this spot as a crybaby bridge, there's quite a story behind the haunting. Well, several stories actually. People disagree on the details.

In most versions of the tale, Theorosa was a young woman who died in Jester's Creek. Some say her husband stabbed her to death and some say she drowned after throwing/dropping her child into the creek (who also, reportedly, perished). The most popular version of the story is that Native Americans abducted her child and she is eternally searching for her missing offspring. Whichever you prefer, it does seem that the bridge is certainly visited by a female apparition.

A quick online search will bring you tales of the apparition, the sighting of spook lights, the sounds of moans/screams and a baby crying, and frigid drafts that seem to appear at random. Strangely enough, the current version of the span is the third to exist here; the previous two incarnations both burned. Hopefully not by the fiery balls of light that people see shooting through the air.

## Boeuf River Bridge—Fiske Union, Louisiana

Finding this particular location may be the scariest part of visiting this bridge. Tucked in the backroads between the towns of Fiske Union, Oak Grove, and Kilbourne, this small bridge over the Boeuf River is said to be plagued with mysterious lights that jaunt down the road, roam the bridge, and even bounce along the waters beneath. Some guess the lights are representative of the headlights of a car that wrecked on the bridge, killing the man and woman inside. Some say the two ghosts just like to appear as balls of light.

Regardless, dozens have reported seeing the spectacle. Other activity at this spot includes the sounds of a male voice moaning, the apparition of a young woman, and even horrible screams. All of this is thought to be remnants of the aforementioned accident, though a few people have claimed that the female spirit is quite intelligent. She is known for approaching cars and even those who are brave enough to exit their vehicle and explore the area. If that isn't creepy enough for you, the story goes that as the woman approaches you, the male voice will switch from moans to whispers advising you to leave the area.

## Puttygut Bridge—China Township, Michigan

It's always nice when a ghost story can be differentiated from an urban legend about an area. Such is the case with this bridge. Located on a backroad close to the Canadian border, legend trippers enjoy watching hapless teens scare themselves silly at this spot.

The story goes that you are supposed to park your car on the bridge, turn it off, and then place your keys on the roof of your car. If you do, the spirit of a man killed in an auto accident will appear and approach your vehicle—sometimes via the road, sometimes crawling up from the water below in the Belle River. While some have claimed to have seen this whole scenario play out for them, the most reliable witnesses have described a completely different and real encounter—that of a ghost light.

Dozens of people, expecting to have a fun night giggling and waiting for a ghost to appear, have seen a perfectly round ball of light bobbing along the road and, usually, disappearing in the nearby woods. A quick search of this site will bring up a lot of forum posts describing this event happening. Could there have been a car accident with a fatality here? Sure. Why not? Could the ghost be appearing sporadically as a spook light versus an apparition? Again, why not? Sort out the truth of this one for yourself.

## Arcola High Bridge—Stillwater, Minnesota

Spanning the St. Croix River between Minnesota and Wisconsin, this gorgeous bridge is comparable to the works of Eiffel in France. Looming 184 feet over the waters below, this bridge is also known as the Soo Line Railroad Bridge. Yes, you read that correctly—a railroad bridge. So don't be making any plans to walk on it—especially since trains still use the tracks there. However, you can certainly visit the river below the bridge and that would make a great spot to keep a lookout for the mysterious blue light that people have been seeing at this locations for decades.

Some say the light is the ghost of a woman (sometimes seen in full apparition form), some say the light is a lantern held by the spirit of a man who used to service the railroad. His ghost has also been seen carrying the same lantern. Whichever version of the story you choose to believe, regular sightings of the light occur. Sometimes the light can be seen high above you on the tracks, sometimes it pops up beneath the bridge. Interestingly, the ruins of an old house are nearby that people have claimed to be the old railroad worker's home—and the blue light has been seen there, too. It all adds up to a pretty interesting haunt. And even if you don't see the spook light, the bridge is an awe-inspiring landmark all on its own.

## Morphus Bridge—Wendell, North Carolina

This bridge has a bit of a twist on the typical ghost light sighting. Rather than bobbing down the road or gliding through the trees, the lights at this site are seen underwater. They are said to be the headlights of a car that drove off the road and ended up in the Little River.

According to the tale, a family was driving home when said accident occurred, killing everyone inside the vehicle. But ghostly headlights are only the beginning of the paranormal activity at this spot. Legend says if you stop your car on the bridge and turn it off, the apparition of a girl will appear. Some say it is the mother that was killed in the accident, some say it's the daughter. Either way, she approaches your vehicle, crying, and tries to get in.

I probably don't have to tell you that it is extraordinarily dangerous to stop a vehicle in the middle of a functioning bridge, but I will anyway. Don't do it. It's dangerous! Settle for staking out the river for the spook lights there. If you see them, maybe you can spot the spirit of the girl on the structure as well.

## Blue Bridge—Huron County, Ohio

The name of this bridge isn't actually Blue Bridge, but the locals all call it that because it is painted blue. And since it really doesn't have any other name, well, we'll keep it! Spanning the Seymour Creek, this bridge is known for mysterious lights that seem to dance around the area and skip across the water. They're said to be just a part of the paranormal activity that happens at this spot—activity that's attributed to Native Americans who were killed during the War of 1812. With several bloody skirmishes that happened in the area (Seymour Creek is named for an Ohio militiaman who was killed here), most believe the lights are the spirits of the dead. Those who have seen the lights say that, on occasion, they are accompanied by chanting, dark figures, and unnatural mists that seem to defy the wind.

The entire region surrounding this tributary of the Huron River is a nature lover's dream. There's plenty to see and do outdoors. So if you make the trip to this bridge on Lamereaux Road, and you don't have a ghostly experience of your own, you will have it made if you brought along your camping gear.

## Fought Road Bridge—Lindsey, Ohio

Sometimes a ghost light is simply a mysterious glow in the night and sometimes there's a neat story that explains that light. Such is the case of this backcountry bridge and the legend of the Elmore Rider. The story goes like this…

There was a young man just back from World War I who was planning to go see the girl he left behind. He had purchased a motorcycle in his hometown of Elmore and was planning a trip to visit her at her place when he learned that she had become engaged to another man while he was deployed. Angry, he drove at breakneck speed to get to her farm. Unfortunately, he did not make it there. He wrecked on the bridge, killing himself instantly.

Now it's said that if you visit the bridge on the evening of March 21, park your car, and then blink your lights three times and honk your horn three times, a mysterious light will appear and shoot across the bridge. This, of course, is supposed to be the headlight of the motorcycle. To make this story even more intriguing, it's said that a ghost hunter by the name of Richard Gill attempted to debunk the Elmore Rider. Not only did he witness the light appear several times, but at one point it knocked one of his co-investigators down.

## Maud Hughes Road Bridge—Middletown, Ohio

Looking at the list of activity and legends associated with this bridge, it could have been placed into almost any chapter of this book. Located between the Ohio towns of Middletown, Fairfield, and Mason, this structure crosses a double set of train tracks that's the source of half the stories about this place. Where to begin?

There's a ghost light that's seen bobbing along the tracks beneath the bridge that's said to be the spirit of a train engineer who died when the boiler blew on his locomotive. Then there are the ghosts that are seen and heard on the bridge itself. They are supposed to be a couple that were mysteriously killed one night; she was found hanging from the bridge, and he was dead in their vehicle. Toss in a crybaby-type spirit (yes, a baby was supposedly thrown off) and a handful of automobile accidents (locals say more than thirty people have died at this spot) and you have a bridge with a lot of stories told about it.

But the signature item of this particular haunting has to be the legendary scream that is heard. It's said to be terrible and something that you never forget once you hear it. Most assume the scream is the woman who was killed and hung off the bridge. This ghostly howl is so well known throughout the state of Ohio that the place is known as Screaming Bridge.

## Hansley Road Bridge—Sugar Grove, Ohio

Originally the site of the Hummel Covered Bridge (some still call the new concrete span at this location by this name), this simple structure crosses Rush Creek and is known for a rather grisly urban legend. It's said that during the 1930s or 1940s, there was a local woman who fell in love with a jerk. He was constantly cruel, talking down to her, belittling her in front of others, etc. Finally, one evening, she had enough. While the two were parked at the covered bridge, the woman pulled out a knife and attacked the man. He fought back, mortally injuring her, but she won the battle. The trophy was his head.

Legend says she staggered to the end of the bridge, head in her hand, where she then collapsed dead. Since that night, people have seen a blue light that appears on the bridge and wanders the creek.

Of course, if you decide to test the legend, you don't have to sit there and wait for the ghost light to appear. There's a ritual you can do to call it. You're supposed to walk to the edge of the bridge and call out the woman's name—and after a few moments the light will appear. Naturally there's no historical record of a dead couple that were found at the Hummel Covered Bridge, so we don't really know the spirit's name. But, no worries, most locals say her name is either Anna or Mary. Give both a shot.

## Ellis Bridge—Zanesville, Ohio

In 1913, a massive flood struck this area of Ohio, killing dozens of people, wiping out roads, and even causing the destruction of several bridges, including this one. Because of this, people say the forlorn spirits of the dead now gather in the area beneath Ellis Bridge. They are seen as a group of lights floating about.

Prior to the famous flood of 1913, though, there was also a young woman who got caught in a flood while crossing the original span here—she was immediately swept away in the deluge and drowned a short distance away. Her spirit was discussed as far back as 1900, and has been, on occasion, seen here at the new incarnation of the bridge. So this spot has had a haunted reputation for quite some time.

This small structure sits near Dam/Lock 11 of the Muskingum River and is now part of a walking trail, so checking out the lights for yourself should pose no problem. Just be sure you don't head out to the trail when it's been raining or any flooding has been reported; this spot doesn't have a very good track record of withstanding such conditions.

## Elk Creek Bridge—Sentinel, Oklahoma

Not much happens around the town of Sentinel, Oklahoma, that everyone doesn't know about, so when word got around that spook lights were appearing at the old bridge outside town (nicknamed 3 Mile Bridge), it became an instant tourist attraction. Of course, more people might actually be drawn to it if it wasn't for the scary story associated with the lights.

The story goes that a cult of devil worshippers used to perform rituals along Elk Creek, and one night something went wrong. They conjured something that was too much for them to handle and the thing killed them all. It's said that the spirits of the cult members now appear as a group of mysterious lights along the creek. In addition to this, people say there are disembodied voices (sometimes chanting, sometimes moans and groans), shadowy figures walking about, and the occasional mangled animal corpse is found. Sounds like the cult is still at it in the afterlife if the reports are true.

Visit this location at your own risk. It's popular with the locals for ghost watching, partying, and general mischief.

## Purple Light Bridge—Elizabethtown, Pennsylvania

This otherwise nameless bridge is known for the weird purple light that seems to float along the train tracks underneath it. Some say the light is a lantern that was held by a railroad worker who was struck and killed while on duty, some say it is the spirit of a young boy who was also killed, and then some say the spirit is a hobo who used to hop trains at this spot and was—you probably guessed it by now—killed. Regardless of who actually died, the purple light is said to dodge people who try to touch it and seems to have intelligence of a sort.

The challenge to checking out this particular spot may be finding Purple Light Bridge. Locals disagree where the place is actually located, but there does seem to be two choices that emerge as the best contenders. The first is the bridge at the intersection of Turnpike Road and West High Street (the Amtrak station is nearby) and the second is a small bridge located close to Bossler Road. Good luck with the search for this bridge, as well as for the purple light.

## Hogback Road Bridge—Hermitage, Pennsylvania

It's always interesting to read the origin stories for spook lights and this one does not disappoint, though it's also wrapped up with a second legend that's not very pleasant. For years people have been seeing a greenish light that seems to bob and weave through the trees in the woods along Hogback Road. People say this light is the lantern that a young woman carried many years ago as she searched for her missing family. She would find them dead beneath this bridge (well, an earlier predecessor anyway) and end up taking her own life. This in itself is an interesting ghost story, but then there's another tale ...

It's also said Hogback Road was a popular place for the Ku Klux Klan (KKK) to lynch people. They would take these poor people to the bridge and hang them from the side. At least one paranormal researcher has even combined the two tales and says that the dead family was hung by the KKK. History does seem to suggest this was a bad area for this kind of activity in the early 1900s, so there's a grain of truth to the story at least (I could find no specific documentation of a murder here).

Sightings of the apparitions under the bridge and the green ghost light now occur regularly. Other activity includes bizarre mists that suddenly appear and odd screams that emanate from the woods. If you're feeling particularly daring, you may want to try the Hogback Dare. Supposedly, if you leave your car keys on the bridge for five minutes and then go try to start your vehicle with them, your car will not work. Since it doesn't involve actually parking on the bridge, it might be an interesting experiment.

## St. John's Road Bridge—Slippery Rock, Pennsylvania

Like many ghost lights scattered around the country, the two bright lights seen traveling down St. John's Road and disappearing at this bridge are said to be the headlights of a car that passed through long ago. Legend states that said car did not fare so well on this road, though. After running into the back of a horse-drawn wagon, the couple within the automobile was instantly killed (nothing is said of the horse or anyone who was in the wagon at the time).

Now these ghostly lights reenact this awful event each night. If you happen to actually be driving down this road when this act occurs, locals say you will even hear the screams of the people just before they hit the wagon and that the headlights will approach your vehicle from behind, disappear for a moment as they pass through your car, then reappear in front of you until they hit the bridge and disappear for good. This may be one of the few times that you can safely have a ghost pass right through you—so enjoy it!

## Crazy George's Bridge—Dry Hollow, Tennessee

Though it isn't the actual name of this bridge, it's as good as any for it (there's no official name for this simple concrete span over the train tracks). It's part of a duo of dares that most everyone that lives in the area knows. It's said a man by the name of George was walking the train tracks when he was struck and killed by a train. Now he appears as a light bobbing along in the area (supposed to be his lantern). In some versions of the story, he was decapitated by the train and is searching for his head.

This is usually the first stop for a night of legend tripping; the second stop would be the nearby Witch's Cemetery. Again, not the actual name of the place. The graveyard is said to be the stomping grounds of witches/spirits. Yes, that's right. Dead witches now haunt the tombstones and scare passersby. This rumor was all started when late 1700s–era headstones were noted to have pentagrams on them. Most everyone agrees that these are present either because the deceased was a soldier or the mark was the signature of the stonemason who made them. But that certainly hasn't stopped anyone from looking for the ghost witches.

## River Legacy Park Bridge—Arlington, Texas

There are actually two odd sets of lights at this site, and both have a link to the horrible story associated with the bridge. In 1961, a car filled with six teenage girls plunged into a ravine here. Three of the girls died; three survived. It turned out the bridge had been burned earlier as a prank. Strangely enough, two more girls would die close by in 1994 when they attempted to beat a train at a crossing. These two very real events are now woven into the ghostly lights that are seen at the bridge.

The first lights are a bit of a stretch; it's said if you look into the water under the bridge, glowing tombstones will appear there with the names of the victims of the 1961 crash. Then there's a set of fairly typical ghost lights that many say are supposed to be the headlights of one of the two cars that wrecked. This set is supposed to bob up the road and disappear upon crossing the bridge. Today, this location is in the middle of River Legacy Park—a place known for their awesome trails. Maybe a hike to the bridge is in order?

## Old Greenhouse Road Bridge—Houston, Texas

It seems that sightings of the paranormal at this location fall into two categories: Spook light or full-blown apparition. But if you want to catch a glimpse of the spirit at this bridge you will need to approach with caution; it's said that if the ghost sees you coming, she will disperse rather quickly.

What you want to do is drive slowly along Old Greenhouse Road until you see the bridge over Bear Creek. If you're lucky, you will see one of two things. You could see a greenish, glowing ball of light that seems to be roaming over the road or across the bridge. Or you could find yourself staring at a misty apparition of an old woman—and if she also sees you, she will scream and disappear.

There are a couple different theories as to who the woman is. Some say she is a witch who has haunted the area since the 1800s; others say she is a mean old lady who died in an auto/carriage accident while crossing the creek. Whoever she is, most who see the apparition in all its glory say that she is quite frightening. Maybe you'll get lucky and just see the spook light version.

## Vietnam Veterans Memorial Bridge—Richmond, Virginia

Constructed in 2002 as part of the Pocahontas Parkway, this span over the James River was a sorely needed bypass for the busy State Route 895 thoroughfare. When it opened, it was met with a huge sigh of relief—followed quickly by occasional gasps of fear. No sooner did this bridge open than people began to see flickering balls of light beneath it. Seemingly intelligent, they roam around however they see fit. But it doesn't stop there. During the day, the lights are replaced with full-blown apparitions that seem to be Native American warriors. At least one pair of witnesses have also reported hearing sounds that obviously are from another time; they were driving the parkway, their windows down, when they began to hear singing/chanting, drums playing, and the various sounds that would accompany a war party on the march.

This is an extremely busy highway, so I wouldn't recommend attempting any kind of investigation along here; however, a nice drive across the James River with your windows down would be perfectly fine.

## Macedonia Road Train Trestle —Buckhannon, West Virginia

The entire stretch of Macedonia Road is thought to be haunted and many are the tales that surround this location. Your best bet for checking these spots out is to find a good spot to park and hike the road—so there's no need to do anything reckless, such as climbing onto a train trestle for instance. The small bridge is known for misty apparitions and spook lights that appear during the dark hours and are said to be the sad spirits of those who died on the nearby Deadman's Curve.

There have been documented deaths from automobile accidents on this road and one researcher has even pointed out that a pedestrian was struck and killed by a car near the trestle. Because of this, the entire road is said to be inhabited with dark figures, spooky disembodied voices, and (much like the train trestle) glowing balls of light that roam the area.

This is one of those spots that it's probably best to let the local sheriff know you are exploring; because of its haunted reputation, a lot of partying and semi-illegal activities occur on Macedonia Road. Be careful!

## Grant Park Covered Bridge—Milwaukee, Wisconsin

While this bridge is certainly known as a haunted spot in South Milwaukee, it's also well known for being the starting point for an entire haunted trail. The Seven Bridges Trail has lots of stories that are told about it, and it's regarded as one of the most visited ghostly spots in the city. According to local folklore, the covered bridge was the site of several suicides that have caused the bridge to now be populated with glowing, sparkling sprite lights. Odd ghost lights have also been spotted along the trail. But that's not all that's there...

Walking the trail at night (something that is actually against the law since the park is closed then) is supposed to be quite the frightening thing. The sounds of laughing and screaming seemingly emanate from the trees, and visitors have complained of hearing something stalking them along the trail. While nothing is actually seen, witnesses say you can hear phantom footsteps, heavy breathing, and guttural growls. Sounds like a spooky trail in a nice park.

## Chapter 10
# UNFORTUNATE ACCIDENTS

While bridges are certainly constructed to assist motorists with a very basic function (crossing a usually impassable location), they are oftentimes also the site of some horrible events. Floods and other natural disasters, as well as auto accidents, can strike a bridge at any time and, unfortunately, people are usually a part of these events. This chapter lists bridges that have stories that are associated with these types of tragedies.

A lot of these listings are wrapped up in historical facts, so that means some very real people lost their lives, whether you believe the paranormal tales associated with these legends or not. The mingling of fact and fiction is, perhaps, more present here in this chapter than any other place in this book. Read on…

## CR & NW Bridge—Chitina, Alaska

While the Kennecott Mine is known as a haunted location in its own right, it was when the Copper River and Northwestern Railway was built (in order to transport copper from the mine) that the town of Chitina became renowned as a haunted place.

The CR & NW is a two-hundred-mile stretch of track that traverses the Alaskan countryside from Kennicott Glacier to Cordova. The construction of this railway was extremely difficult—with workers often having to blast their way through cliffs and rock ranges in order to continue building. Because of this, it's estimated that dozens died while the tracks were built. And of the many haunted places associated with the railway, the old Chitina River Bridge is the most notorious.

When the state of Alaska contemplated renovating the old railway in the 1990s, tales of ghosts began circulating fast. It's said that workers would often hear odd voices, see mysterious tombstones along the tracks, and even see the occasional apparition as it scooted along. Even today, visitors to the small town of Chitina (the 2010 census placed the population there at 126) are said to have the occasional encounter with the spirits of the old CR & NW.

## Cotter Bridge—Cotter, Arkansas

Constructed in 1930, the Cotter Bridge spans the White River (a location known for the infamous White River Monster) along US Route 62. A few years back it was proposed by the city of Cotter that the bridge be replaced—but because of the history and legends associated with the bridge, locals heavily protested demolition. Of course it is the legends associated with the bridge that we are interested in.

There are two accidents associated with the bridge—one documented by the local paper, one falling more into the realm of urban legend—and either (or both) may have contributed to the haunting that occurs there now. The first story concerns two men who were working on the bridge; they were high on the structure performing some repairs when they fell to their death. The second incident is a little shadier, but well known in Cotter. Sometime during the 1950s, a young woman was chased across the bridge by a pack of wild dogs. It's said she was torn apart on the bridge and now she is seen there in the dark hours. But neither of these stories account for all of the odd activity at the bridge.

Those who have had encounters here have reported hearing the odds sounds of children playing under the bridge (though, obviously, there are none there in the middle of the night) and even the bizarre crying of an infant. Other activity is, however, consistent with the stories: The sounds of footsteps/walking on the bridge, odd (adult) disembodied voices, and even the occasional sighting of a female spirit.

## Santa Margarita Bridge—Fallbrook, California

Though this bridge in Fallbrook is known for two separate hauntings, it is primarily the story of a terrible accident that brings out the adventurous (but don't worry, both tales will be told here).

During the infamous Gold Rush of California, thousands of pioneers streamed into the area looking to make their fortunes—and it's no surprise that many accidents happened involving these individuals rushing to make a claim. It's said that just such an accident occurred at this location. Two covered wagons were hustling to make their way to the gold when they hurtled against one another, ending with the deaths of those aboard. Today, visitors to the Santa Margarita River have been seeing the spirits of these poor souls.

If that isn't enough, a second story (of murder no less) is told that involves the horrible deaths of six students who were on their way to attend prom at the local high school. According to this legend, the teens were missed at the dance and a search was formed to find them. They were later found—all dead—in the river. Much like the pioneers, people have claimed to see and hear these spirits in the vicinity of the bridge.

## San Francisco-Oakland Bay Bridge —San Francisco, California

Built from 1933 to 1936 to connect the communities of San Francisco and Berkeley/Oakland, this famous bridge opened six months before the even more famous Golden Gate Bridge. Today it carries an average of 240,000 automobiles/commuters a day. Among those commuters are the curious who hope to catch a glimpse of what may be one of the most reliably spotted ghosts in history.

The background of the tale involves a man circa 1940s who was apparently struck and killed on the bridge after his car broke down. In the present day, the spirit of this man in his rumpled coat and fedora is seen almost daily. Almost everyone in the area has a tale, or a friend who has a tale, about the apparition. Most stories say the ghost is only visible from the corner of your eye—and that he disappears when you turn to look directly at him. Of course he isn't the only phantom seen on the span...

In what seems an even more morbid accident, the spirit of a headless person is often seen running along the bridge. It has been proposed that this ghost is the product of the 1989 earthquake—and this entity has been blamed for the sounds of knocks on passing cars on the lower deck. The apparition with the head is seen on the upper span of the bridge just as you exit the Yerba Buena Island Tunnel, the headless one is usually spotted on the eastern half of the bridge.

## Scott's Run Bridge—St. George's, Delaware

Locals know this basic concrete bridge on Route 13 as Fiddler's Bridge, and if you weren't ghost hunting and looking for it, you'd pass right over it without giving it a second glance. While it certainly isn't much of a bridge, the legend about the span is quite interesting.

The story dates back to the late 1800s/early 1900s and has been told around campfires for generations. It goes like this: There once was a small plantation in the area where a young African-American slave lived. He was known far and wide as a master fiddle player, but he would often get in trouble for shirking his duties to play the instrument. Once, after a particularly brutal beating, the slave suffered brain damage and became unable to work at the plantation. As a result, he moved into a small shack on the property and took to wandering at night with his violin. This went on until one evening when he fell into Scott's Run and drowned.

Since that accident, people have stated that you can visit the bridge over the creek and hear the sad fiddle music play at night. But there is a catch... To have the best odds of encountering this spirit—and hearing his spectral music—you need to visit the bridge at midnight. And you need to bring some change. Yes, you read that correctly. According to legend, you need to stand on the bridge at the right time, then drop a coin into the water. If you do this, it's said the spirit will begin to play you a tune, just like a ghostly jukebox.

## St. Johns River Veterans Memorial Bridge
### —Lake Monroe, Florida

It sounds like something from a horror movie: A road/bridge is built over the graves of four local settlers and bad things ensue! But this seems to be the exact legend associated with this particular location. According to a local historian, accidents were bound to happen when cars began driving across the dead—and it does seem to be the case.

An article by the *Orlando Sentinel* places approximately forty-four accidents on this stretch of road between 1995 and 1997. That's just two years! Although efforts to place a historical marker for the graves have been in vain, most acknowledge that there was an old community at the spot called St. Joseph.

As for the ghost sightings at this bridge…is it a result of the unhappy dead buried in the asphalt covered graves or the result of one of the accidents that have occurred over the years? Your guess is as good as mine, but witnesses to the activity say a dark shadowy shape likes to hang out in the area and voices crying out in the night have been heard. If you don't have any luck chasing this particular spirit, stick around and check out the gorgeous Lake Monroe nearby.

## Train Trestle Bridge—Melbourne, Florida

First off, a warning is in order here. This bridge is a working railroad crossing over the alligator-infested Crane Creek. So do not attempt to walk on or cross this bridge! Add in the fact that this location has a sad and tragic past of pedestrian deaths and you should consider yourself amply warned.

It is this history with death that has locals talking about ghosts at this location. It's said the earliest deaths date back to 1920s and that, all told, at least ten people have been killed here. The most recent accident involved three teenage girls in 2010, who were struck as they attempted to cross the span on foot. According to news reports, a similar incident occurred in 1992. Oddly enough, locals claim that certain people simply cannot hear when a train is crossing the tracks—almost like the environment purposefully masks the sounds. According to one witness (of paranormal events, not the tragic accidents), who claims to be psychically sensitive, the entire area around the trestle emits a negative aura. Many others simply say the place is evil and that it draws bad things to it, such as the alligators looking for a meal. Activity at this location includes balls of light seen on the tracks and under the bridge, as well as the occasional apparition moaning in the night.

## White's Bridge—Colquitt, Georgia

This small bridge spanning Spring Creek has had quite a reputation over the years for ghost sightings. Neighbors in the area will be happy to spin you the tale concerning these ghosts—but why do that when you can read it right here?

According to legend, a family was in a hurry to get home during a particularly bad thunderstorm when their horse and carriage approached White's Bridge. Because of flooding, lack of railing, and poor visibility, the crossing did not go so well. The wife and a child were thrown into the creek below, with the child being swept away in the waters. Today, the woman is said to be seen in this area wailing and searching for her missing baby.

Interestingly, a second story is also associated with this spot. In this version, the young lady who is seen wandering the bridge and creek is a victim of suicide. After discovering her father had murdered her fiancé, the girl killed herself by jumping from the bridge and drowning in the creek below. Either way, the spirit of the girl has been seen a lot at this location and she is almost always accompanied by the sounds of crying.

Legend also states that staring into the waters below the bridge at sunset will allow you to see the spectral tombstone of the dead—and if you happen to see a floating lantern of light, you may be seeing her approach.

## Camp Creek Trestle—McDonough, Georgia

This particular haunting is based entirely on a true and horrible event that took place on June 23, 1900. A train carrying passengers from the station in McDonough, bound for Atlanta, encountered a trestle over Camp Creek that had been nearly destroyed by recent flooding. The engineer attempted to halt the train, but he could not. The trestle collapsed under the weight of the train, sending it and the bridge into the waters below. Thirty-five people died in the accident, ten survived. Today, the location of the accident can be seen from Highway 42, but if you want to see the ghosts you will have to go to downtown McDonough to the old square.

While claims of ghosts have been reported at the old trestle, most of the spirits seem to be in the locations where the bodies were laid out, and where people later died from the wounds sustained in the wreck. The entirety of the square has its share of stories about these specters, but the bulk of the tales involve the sites of the old Globe Hotel and the Season's Bistro, where locals say the funeral home once existed that handled all the burials of the dead.

## Carver Mill Bridge—Pickens County, Georgia

If you're driving along Carver Mill Road in rural Georgia you will eventually find yourself crossing a small paved bridge perched over Scarecorn Creek. At one time, this span was actually made of wood—flimsy wood, it would seem. According to local yarns, an automobile was crossing said bridge sometime during the 1950s or so when the bridge collapsed. The accident killed the young couple inside the car, and it's said that the man decided to stick around.

But you have to perform the associated ritual if you want to see his ghost. It goes like this: If you drive your car onto this bridge and then turn off all the lights inside and outside of the car (headlights, dome lights, flashlights, etc.), the shadowy form of the gentleman will appear walking toward your vehicle. It's said he will first approach the side that contains any women who are inside. Presumably, this is because his own wife was killed in the accident and he wants to get other women off the bridge.

As the story goes, the man will continue circling the vehicle until you drive off or turn on the lights. Locals suggest visiting this spot on a night with a full moon so you can see better. It's debatable if this is a good thing or a bad thing…

## Avon Bridge—Avon, Indiana

This fully functional railroad bridge has been a curiosity for visitors for decades. Find any list of active, haunted places in Indiana and you will find this old trestle. Dating back to the early 1900s, this bridge serviced the Central Pacific Railroad, and was a vital connection between the two sides of White Lick Creek. It wasn't terribly long after its construction that tales of a ghost—possibly two—started circulating the area.

The first haunted tale is lesser known and involves a construction worker falling to his death. Reputedly this was during the building of the bridge and his ghost can now be seen walking the train tracks. The second, and most well-known story, concerns the spirit of a forlorn mother. It's said she was walking the tracks, carrying her infant who was sick, attempting to get to a local doctor's residence, when a train suddenly appeared. She attempted to run but could not get across the bridge fast enough. So she jumped. The infant was killed immediately, but the woman lived long enough to mourn the loss before finally succumbing to either grief or her wounds.

People who have had paranormal experiences at this bridge say that her moans and wails can be heard under the bridge where she and her baby fell. As mentioned above, this is a working train bridge, so you do not want to walk on it. And, as it turns out, you don't have to. The Avon-Washington Township Park is right below the structure and it makes a great spot to wait for the spooky sounds to kick in.

## Tunnel Mill Road Bridge—Charlestown, Indiana

This basic span crossing Fourteen Mile Creek is known to ghost hunters in the area as Ten Penny Bridge. Based on a local urban legend, the structure has an associated ritual that has been tested by almost every high school student in the surrounding region. The story goes that you need to take ten pennies with you to the bridge, park your vehicle, and then place the pennies in a straight line along the bridge's entrance. This act summons the spirit of a homeless man who was struck down and killed by an automobile at this spot.

You will know the trick is working when electric items stop working; flashlights go out, your car won't start, and wrist watches go awry. It's said that, at this point, if you check on the pennies, you will find that they have scattered all over the bridge. Normally, this is the end of the ghostly activity. However, a few witnesses have also thrown in a couple additional details to the haunt. The spirit will sometimes touch those on the bridge and some have heard a strange, whispering voice—as if the ghost is trying to say something in your ear. Head out to Tunnel Mill Road and check it out. It only costs ten cents.

## Colville Covered Bridge—Bourbon County, Kentucky

Close to the town of Paris, this magnificent structure is one of only four covered bridges in the state that is still open to vehicular traffic. It was built in 1877 and has managed to stick around despite being damaged multiple times by floods over the years. Several Internet-famous paranormal types have investigated this haunted spot—and the authenticity of the spirit there is staunchly defended by a few of these folks. A couple different explanations have been put forth about the source of the ghost; some say it was the result of an auto accident that claimed the life of a young lady, some say a pair of teens drowned in the cold waters beneath the bridge. Either way, the apparition of a girl has been seen on the bridge, odd voices have been heard, and (to support the idea of the auto accident) mysterious headlights are said to often approach vehicles that park on the span during the night. Of course, the headlights are supposed to disappear before the ghostly vehicle pulls in behind you.

Ghost or not, this covered bridge is a historic landmark and well worth the visit. It's also located in the middle of bourbon country, so there's plenty to see in the region associated with that particular beverage if you're so inclined.

## Middle Bridge—Warren County, Kentucky

Located along Middle Bridge Road, this old structure has a lot of campfire tales associated with it. The most well-told story involves the supposed sister of a local man named Milton Hancock. Uncle Milt, a legend in his own right, is known for his BBQ skills back in the day. Apparently his sister was swimming in Drake's Creek when she turned up missing. A search was formed and the girl was eventually found drowned in the water. Most believe she now haunts the area surrounding the bridge.

Of course there is an alternate story, too—one that's a bit more nefarious. This version puts the girl on the bridge with a small group of people, having a great time, until she is raped and killed by several male students from the local university. Whichever one you lean toward, the ghost of the young girl has been seen and heard here. At least one witness has claimed that the spirit will actually approach your car and crawl on the hood—if you stop. So you may not want to stop.

## Ghost Bridge—Winchester, Kentucky

Known for miles around as Ghost Bridge, this nondescript structure in the area of Van Meter Road is a popular dare for high school kids in the area. Legend states that a group of four male teenagers were out for a fun evening when they stopped at the old bridge to do some drinking and partying. After a few beers, the merriment turned into a bit of bragging and a few dares were thrown around. This led to the group of guys jumping together off the bridge. None of them survived, but all four of them live on as ghosts!

People who have taken up the dare to hunt the spirits say you can see black, human-shaped figures walking around beneath the bridge. Others have reported hearing disembodied voices (including the four of them yelling as they jump), feeling cold spots, and even seeing at least one of the boys standing at the end of the bridge. Most say the entire affair is rather tame, but a few folks have said that the experience is quite frightening. An amateur investigator in Kentucky stated that she almost passed out when she saw the dark masses under the structure and an eerie moan was heard on the wind.

## Adrian Train Trestle—Adrian, Michigan

Most locals know this trestle outside of town, so you may want to ask directions before attempting to find it (it appears to be off a dirt road between the towns of Adrian and Sand Creek). You may also want to use caution if you visit this site; it is a functioning set of train tracks, so do not walk on the tracks. Besides, you don't need to be on the trestle to look for the ghost at this spot.

Legend says a farmhouse once stood nearby and that tragedy struck that place many years ago. Apparently the house caught fire and the family quickly evacuated the premises. The man of the house attempted to shepherd his animals into the nearby barn away from the blaze while the lady of the house and their child ran to the train tracks to flag down an approaching locomotive. Unfortunately, the train could not stop for the two on the tracks and they were struck and killed. Some even state that the farmer perished in the barn, along with the animals, after the fire spread in that direction.

Today, people claim to see the specter of the poor farmer wandering the area, searching for his family. As mentioned, the train tracks are functioning—and the neighboring areas are all private property—so use caution when visiting here and be respectful of the neighbors.

## Crawford Road Bridge—Cass City, Michigan

Legend states this bridge is the site of a gruesome nineteenth-century accident. The story goes that a lady was driving her horse and buggy along when one of her wagon wheels slipped off the edge of the bridge. The entire contraption flipped over into the water below, trapping the woman until she drowned.

Now, if you drive along the bridge and stop, you are supposed to hear the woman begin begging for help. And, if you're lucky, you might even see her clamber up over the side of the bridge and approach your vehicle. If you decide to check this location out, you may want to check out a couple other things as well…

Apparently Crawford Road no longer connects to the bridge, so you will have to do some walking if you want to see the site. Also, it may be private property that you have to cross in order to get to the bridge, so you may want to check with local authorities to confirm this. The only thing worse than having a scary, wet ghost woman approach you (screaming no less), would be having a couple police officers approach you with a nice, big trespassing ticket in their hands.

## George Brett Bridge—Kansas City, Missouri

Perhaps the most amazing thing about this bridge is that the new incarnation was built in a mere seventy-five days and still managed to open twenty-four hours earlier than expected. The old bridge at this location was demolished in January 2011, just after the end of the Kansas City Chiefs football season, and the new bridge was built in the days leading up to the opening of the Kansas City Royals baseball season. And speaking of Royals…

The structure is named for one of the Royals' all-time greats George Brett, and, believe it or not, the bridge is said to be haunted by a male spirit that was a Royals fan. The story goes that during the infamous I-70 World Series in 1985 a fan was celebrating the Royals win over the St. Louis Cardinals when he was struck by a drunk motorist in the vicinity of the bridge. Now that man wanders the bridge, still wearing his Royals cap.

Realizing, of course, that this tale was spun during the life span of the previous bridge, people say the ghost is still around. Sightings of the man have been documented as recently as 2014. So, unless you are a Cardinals fan, you may want to take a trip to KC and keep an eye out for one of the Royals' most die-hard followers.

## Phelps Grove Park Bridge—Springfield, Missouri

Located in the middle of a city park (Phelps Grove Park on Bennett Street), this bridge is just one more draw for people who visit there. It's associated with the legend of the Bride Ghost that people have claimed to see for quite a few years now. The tale states that a young married couple was having an argument when their horse-drawn carriage suddenly flipped over, killing both of them. Since the accident occurred, the apparition of the young bride has been appearing at the bridge. Well, under the bridge actually. Locals say she likes to show up at sunset or early evening and can be seen with her wedding dress and veil on.

This haunting is a bit on the tame side since the appearance is pretty much all there is to the event. But, hey, the park has trails, baseball fields, and tennis courts, and even a playground with picnic tables and BBQ grills. So there's plenty to do during the day while you're waiting for the sun to go down. Even if you don't see the spirit it sounds like it would be a nice day trip.

## Black Bridge—Nashua, New Hampshire

The stories concerning this infamous train trestle are a perfect example of fact and fiction blending to make urban legend. The legend states that ghostly children haunt the area surrounding this bridge and the waters of the Nashua River below because of a massive train derailment in the 1950s. The reality is that there was a derailment in 1954, but it occurred at the train station (a distance away) and there was only one fatality—a woman by the name of Mary Buckley—not a child, much less multiple children.

Unfortunately, there are also a few other facts that should be mentioned about this train crossing. Over the years there have been several deaths associated with the structure, all thought to be either suicides or accidents that happened when someone foolishly decided to try and walk the trestle. Don't be one of these fatalities! It's okay to stake out the bridge from the safety of the river, but train trestles are dangerous things.

As for the ghosts at this site—well, people say they hear children that aren't there. But they also say an apparition of a man has been seen, too. Perhaps the product of one of the known deaths, witnesses say the ghost stares at anyone who notices him and then disappears.

## Combs Hollow Road Bridge—Mendham, New Jersey

This small town in New Jersey has been the home to such notables as Peter Dinklage, Whitney Houston, and Abner Doubleday. It's the kind of small town that's full of history and not much else. Of course, you could take a drive out to Combs Hollow Road around midnight to see if you can catch a glimpse of the apparition that's said to appear on the bridge…

The story goes that a man was driving home when he struck and killed a female pedestrian on the bridge. Distraught, he fled the scene to his nearby home—and after realizing the extent of his situation, he then committed suicide. Now his spirit returns to the site of his ghastly misfortune. Those who have seen the specter on the bridge say that you must drive there at midnight for him to appear. Perhaps this was the time the hit-and-run occurred or maybe he only shows up for a bit at the beginning of each new day. The ghost is said to be standing and gazing at the bridge when he shows up. Almost as if he's contemplating the terrible thing that once happened here.

## Mill Street Bridge—Angola, New York

This railroad bridge is associated with a horrific event known as the Angola Horror. It was December 1867 when a train en route to Buffalo derailed at this location. Part of the locomotive fell into Big Sister Creek below, part of it burned (the cars were made of wood and used kerosene lamps for lighting). The results were fifty dead and more than a hundred injured. It was a traumatic event that generations of locals still talk about today; of course, one of the reasons they are still talking has everything to do with the ghost stories now associated with the bridge, as well as another legend that seems loosely connected…

Naturally, the haunting is due to the sheer amount of people who were killed in the accident. People have heard disembodied voices/cries on the bridge and even glimpsed the occasional misty figure. This would be scary enough reason to check out this bridge (from afar since it is for trains), but there's a road nearby that should probably make your itinerary, too. It's called Holland Road, but legend trippers have dubbed it Pigman's Road.

The story goes that a butcher once lived in the area and would ward off others using pig heads staked outside his property. When three teens trespassed, it was the final straw for Pigman. He decapitated them, placed their heads on stakes, and hung their bodies from the bridge. Because of this, some think the haunting of the bridge has more to do with Pigman than it does the Angola Horror. Interestingly, some have surmised that the train derailment may have happened because of the maliciousness of Pigman.

## Fiddler's Bridge—Clinton Corners, New York

Here's a haunted bridge that's so popular that they named the street after it. Take a drive down Fiddler's Bridge Road and you will come across this legendary site standing alone in the mists—just like the lost reveler did when he fell to his demise there.

The story goes that a man was walking home from a Halloween party (where he was entertaining guests by playing his fiddle) when he hit a patch of fog. Unable to see, he stepped right off the bridge and plummeted to his death. Now, if you drive across the bridge on Halloween night, roll down your windows, and listen closely, you will hear what sounds like a ghostly fiddle playing in the distance. At least one person has claimed to see the apparition of the man, actually in the act of playing his instrument, there on the bridge as well.

This story is very well known throughout New England and the small town of Clinton Corners has had quite a bit of tourism over the Halloween season because of the tale. If you're not busy trick-or-treating, you may consider spending Samhain listening for the ghostly music.

## Troy Country Club Road Bridge—Troy, New York

Spanning the Poestenkill Creek, this bridge is near the private country club that this road is named for. There's not much to say about this nondescript structure other than the ghost story detailed here. It's said that, during a particularly bad winter (and upstate New York is sort of known for these), a waitress who worked for the country club was on her way home when her car slid on the ice and wiped out on the bridge. She was killed instantly and her apparition has been seen ever since.

Locals say when the snow is falling you will see mysterious footprints appear in the area around the bridge and that her apparition is often seen standing, looking lost. I could get no confirmation that any death actually occurred at the bridge, but the ghost story is pretty much available all over the Internet. This is pretty typical with urban legends, but as I stated in the introduction of the book, sometimes a ghost story is made up to account for ghostly activity at a location. You will have to take a trip to the bridge and see for yourself if it is truly haunted.

## Craven Street Bridge—Asheville, North Carolina

Asheville is a city that loves its ghost stories. Don't believe me? Just give it a Google. Dozens of haunted tales are told about various points of the city, as well as the surrounding area—and there's even a top-notch haunted tour you can take there. As for the legend surrounding the Craven Street Bridge...Well, there's not much known.

For years, people have been claiming to see the apparition of a small, naked boy either on the bridge or along the bank of the French Broad River. Most surmise that he drowned close to the span and is now wandering, lost forever. During the early days of the city, the waterway was pretty much the center of a lot of industry—trading, fishing, etc.—and, certainly, people depended on the river for many things. So it's entirely possible that this boy met his demise some time ago when the city was less than modernized. But, theories aside, no information about the dead boy in question is to be had—and it really isn't needed. Take a walk through lovely Asheville and maybe you, too, will catch a glimpse of this sad spirit.

## Brubaker Covered Bridge—Preble County, Ohio

This awesome covered bridge was constructed in 1887 by Everett S. Sherman. It's eighty-five feet long and still offers vehicles a safe crossing over Sandy Run. The ghost story concerning this location has been circulating the area since the 1930s. Apparently, a group was on its way home when there was an accident on (or close to) the bridge. Several people were killed and now they plague people who visit the bridge. What do they do? Well, there's the usual stuff: Your car will die, you will hear knocking on the vehicle, and catch the faint sounds of voices whispering. Then there's the unusual stuff...

One version of the Brubaker story states that thirteen people were killed in the accident, but only twelve bodies were found. Now Mr. Thirteen haunts the area. He wants his body to be found and likes to drop hints that he's still around by knocking on your car thirteen times. In this rather drastic version of the tale (I wonder what kind of vehicle in the 1930s could carry thirteen people), the whispers heard are actually angry mumbles. Since the body was never recovered, it decomposed. And now the ghost has no tongue. Makes sense, right?

## Dug Hill Road Bridge—Wapakoneta, Ohio

The first thing you are going to say (or at least think) when you see this bridge is, "Wow, is this the world's tiniest bridge ever?" Seriously, it must be a whopping twelve feet long. But you know what they say: Big things come in little packages. Unfortunately, that saying is way off base in this case.

There is supposed to be a ghost at this bridge, but apparently he only shows up at midnight. He's supposed to be the spirit of a woodsman who was out on a hunt when he was accidentally shot and killed by another hunter. I have no idea what kind of game they were tracking at midnight, but now the irritated apparition is said to chase people off his bridge when they intrude upon his favorite hunting spot. In addition to guarding the bridge, people have also heard bizarre moans and groans from the specter, as well as felt cold spots on the span. You don't like to run, you say? You don't want to be chased? Don't worry, the bridge is only twelve feet long.

## Y-Bridge—Zanesville, Ohio

When you're reading about this three-way bridge (it crosses the confluence of the Licking and Muskingum Rivers) you can't help but be impressed with the history behind it. It's best if we take this chronologically ...

The first Y-Bridge was built in 1814 and managed to last four years before it collapsed. It was replaced a year later, and that incarnation managed to stand until 1832, when it was condemned. It simply could not handle the heavy traffic. The third version of the bridge was quickly built and it lasted until 1900. Number four opened with no fanfare in 1902 and stood for a good spell, but the inevitable number five was planned when this version also became unsafe in 1979.

Today's Y-Bridge opened in 1984. As for the ghosts, they date back a bit. During the construction of the third bridge, a flood caused complications that ended with the bridge collapsing and two men, Ebenezer Buckingham and Jacob Boyd, dying. The spirits of these two are now said to be seen by passersby. In addition to this, people say a ghostly carriage crosses the bridge on occasion, too. It's supposed to belong to Dr. Isaac Fowler, a man who perished when his carriage fell into the river.

## Summit Cut Bridge—Beaver County, Pennsylvania

This relatively new bridge was erected in 1976 as a bypass for the railroad tracks that are located beneath it. Located on Shenango Road, a country lane that weaves and bobs through the forested hills, it's the kind of nondescript span that you'd normally blow by without thinking about it. But if you happen to notice a glowing woman dressed in white walking along the road, well, you just might give it a second look.

Supposedly the lone fatality in an auto accident that happened in the 1980s, the ghostly girl has been sighted here many times. It's said she drove off the structure during a rainy evening, so your chances of spotting the apparition increase during a storm (though your visibility may decrease). Additional activity at this location includes dark figures, small spook lights (sometimes referred to as sprite lights), and odd misty shapes.

Be careful investigating this particular spot; traffic is sporadic and can catch you off guard, streetlights are minimal, and the bridge provides very little in the way of a shoulder. So consider parking a distance away and simply staking out the area for your ghost adventures.

## McConnell's Mill Covered Bridge —Lawrence County, Pennsylvania

Covering more than 2,500 acres, this historic park is known for its circa 1852 gristmill, phenomenal outdoor activities, and this beautiful covered bridge. Dating back to 1874, this is one of two remaining covered bridges in Lawrence County, and it is situated within the park. While this structure is quite extraordinary, the ghost story associated with it is not so much. Pretty standard haunted bridge fare really. The tale concerns a young girl who died in an accident (nothing is specified, but locals say auto accident) who now appears if you park on the bridge and honk your horn three times.

It's pure urban legend and a risky one at that since parking on operational bridges is not such a great idea. However, when stacked up with the other ghost stories concerning this park, it does make for a great haunted day trip. The ghost of a former gristmill worker is often spotted walking along the road—presumably reenacting his trip to work—and the spirit of a caretaker named Moses Whorton has also been spotted roaming the region surrounding the mill.

If that's not enough to make this a ghostly getaway, then also consider that the woods themselves are said to be haunted with the numerous souls claimed by the rugged cliffs and torrential waters of Slippery Rock Creek.

## Slateford Trestle—Mount Bethel, Pennsylvania

This old train trestle rarely, if ever, has trains on it any more (though you shouldn't take any chances). Located just off Slateford Road and the Delaware River, this spot has a well-known haunt. It's said that during the span's construction a worker managed to fall into wet concrete being poured for one of the supports. He was completely submerged and the other workers could not get him free before he suffocated and died. Witnesses say that if you park along the road and watch the trestle, you will see what looks like a black figure/apparition on it. He's also been spotted walking the train tracks leading up to the trestle.

It's great that you can stake this place out from afar; attempting to walk on train bridges is quite dangerous. A dead man was found on this particular trestle in 2014, and over the years there have been even more injured at this spot. A good pair of binoculars were made for haunts like this.

## White River Railroad Bridge
## —West Hartford, Vermont

It was Saturday, February 5, 1887, when a train on the way to Montreal derailed at this spot, hurtling into the ice-covered river. It's estimated that some forty-odd souls were lost in the accident—but it seems that only one has decided to stick around. The young boy's spirit has been dubbed Joe McCabe by locals; some surmise that he was killed in the train wreck, others say his family died here, but his lonely soul is looking for them. Either way, his apparition has been seen and heard playing in the river or sometimes just wandering the riverbank.

One vivid eyewitness account tells of feeling a cold blast that hit her just before a spooky giggle filled the air. When she turned around at the sound of the laugh, she saw a young boy in old-time clothes walking along the edge of the water—only he was floating three feet off the ground. This also purportedly happened during the day. Your best bet to catch a glimpse of this one would be to find a nice cozy spot along the river where you can enjoy a lovely picnic and, possibly, a ghost sighting.

## Purdy Bridge—Purdy, Washington

Spanning 550 feet between Henderson Bay and Burley Lagoon, this bridge was built in 1937 and is listed on the National Register of Historic Places. When it was constructed, it was the longest continuous box girder bridge in the country—and that, in itself, has made the place a tourist attraction. That and the sad ghost story attached to it.

There's not much info about the specter; people in the area say the spirit is a little boy who was struck and killed while attempting to cross the bridge on foot. His apparition is often seen darting across the road to disappear upon reaching the other side. Nobody knows who the boy is, but they say the tragedy occurred sometimes in the 1970s. So keep a sharp eye if you're crossing here and you may catch a glimpse of this pint-sized ghost.

## Weary Road Bridge—Evansville, Wisconsin

The haunting of this bridge is the least of the tales concerning this stretch of bizarre road. Legend states a young man was car surfing along Weary Road when the car hit a bump on the bridge, hurling the man to his death. Now he is seen on the bridge—sometimes as an apparition of a man, sometimes as a glowing light.

But as I just mentioned, there's so much more to Weary Road. First there's the tale of Old Man Weary. Said to be a man who lived nearby, he has been accused of abducting and killing kids and also of being a victim himself of a house fire (along with his children). Some say you can see his glowing apparition standing in the road. Tales of phantom vehicles screaming down this stretch are also told, as well as sightings of shadow people along the sides of the road. If that's not enough for you, there are also sightings of things the locals call imps. They are said to scuttle among the trees, scratch people, and make terrible screeches that are terrifying to hear.

There's a lot going on here, but be careful making this trek into the Wisconsin countryside. Weary Road is also known for underage drinking, vandalism, and general mischief. Have fun!

## Chapter Eleven
# UNACCOUNTED ODDITIES

Sometimes the story about a bridge is so bizarre that it doesn't really fit into any typical category. Sometimes there are multiple tales told about a single place—or at least several different types of paranormal activity. When a location falls into either of these groups, it gets listed here.

With more and more people studying the paranormal, we are starting to understand that there is sometimes a fine line that separates different types of activity. What some people think of as being an evil event, others see as a simple attempt by a ghost to get some attention. Also, consider a location like a witch bridge. A witch is spooky, presumably, because they did some sort of black magic while living. But now that witch is dead, right? So she is a ghost. Or would she be considered a creature since many would regard her as a type of Halloween monster? You get my point. Enjoy reading these listings that, happily, fall between the cracks...

## Refuge Bridge—Clanton, Alabama

This is a bridge story that could have been placed in several chapters of this book. Primarily known for the appearance of mysterious balls of light (also known as ghost lights), Refuge Bridge is a well-documented and regularly visited hotspot for paranormal activity. A quick Google search will bring up quite a few ghost hunters who have visited this location. But the haunting doesn't stop with a few simple lights…

The female spirit that is said to haunt this bridge is known as a malevolent entity. She will often appear on the bridge and pursue those she sees. In addition, she will often appear as a vaguely humanlike black mass that will circle vehicles parked on the bridge and even attempt to enter them. Additional activity includes the sounds of a woman moaning/panting, the discovery of handprints on vehicles, and the ever-present sense that someone is walking alongside you as you are making your way across.

## Creek Park Bridge—La Mirada, California

Creek Park is approximately twenty-six acres of green situated along the La Mirada flood control channel. It features an open-air amphitheater, an equestrian arena, and a pair of spirits that are said to be the remnants of a Satanic ritual.

The ghosts in question are usually spotted in the vicinity of a small wooden bridge that's perched near a popular hiking trail. If you find the bridge, hang tight and keep your eyes open. Locals say the first spirit—that of a young girl—can be seen nearby. She's often heard crying out for her mother. The second ghost is a little spookier; the hooded figure (thought to be male) is usually seen approaching the bridge or skulking about nearby.

Legend says that both entities are the product of a ritual that was carried out in the park sometime in the 1970s, and that both were victims who were sacrificed during the affair. Though they both seem to be a bit residual, and tend to avoid the living, those who have witnessed the apparitions say they are terrifying and have a vivid memory of the event.

## San Lorenzo River Trestle—Santa Cruz, California

Though this bridge is known for an unusual—and malevolent—spirit that haunts it, this trestle is also quite famous for something else entirely. The movie *The Lost Boys* used this bridge for filming a portion of a scene that involves the vampires having a contest to see who can hang the longest beneath the bridge. People visit the bridge from far and wide because of this, but on occasion, visitors leave with an altogether different story…

Unlike most train trestles, this one was constructed with a pedestrian walkway so locals and tourists could cross. It's while taking a stroll across that people have come into contact with the spirit here. According to the local tale, the entity on the trestle is quite evil and will psychically project thoughts into pedestrians' minds, suggesting that they jump off the bridge. Those who have encountered this ghost have even claimed to have seen the thing in their mind speaking to them. Descriptions place the spirit somewhere between ghost and demon—but wearing a hat. Other encounters with the thing have left witnesses shaken up a bit; apparently the evil entity also enjoys giving a push to some people who are making the crossing.

## Veterans Memorial Bridge—Daytona, Florida

There isn't much known about the mysterious spirit that's said to haunt the north side of this bridge. The original span at this location was constructed in 1899, but it was replaced in 1954 to upgrade this crossing of the Halifax River. And it was about this time that the whispers concerning a ghost started circulating the area.

Witnesses of the activity say the entity is a female with dark hair who is wearing a nightgown or, perhaps, robes of some kind. This in itself is reason enough for ghost hunters to check out the area—but what makes this particular spirit odd is that she apparently likes to levitate and move objects. Though nobody has reported actually seeing the apparition throwing things, plenty of locals have claimed to have seen rocks, roadside debris, and other objects fly through the air, seemingly by themselves. And since there is an actual ghost that has been seen here, well, she takes the blame for this activity. While this may seem like a dangerous ghost, investigators in the area say she is not malevolent at all but is simply trying to get the attention of those passing by on her bridge.

## Arbuckle Creek Bridge—Lorida, Florida

It's hard to say what's weirder—the story about this bridge in Highlands County or the fact that the closest town is called Lorida. Yes, that's right—Lorida, Florida. Apparently the original name of the town (Istokpoga) was similar to another in the state, so the name was changed in 1937. That bit of history aside, the tales concerning this area, and this bridge, are squarely in the realm of urban legend—a legend about a witch.

It's said an old woman lived nearby in the woods sometime in the 1940s, and she was known for hundreds of miles as a person who could make remedies, potions, spells, etc. As a result, a gentleman who was interested in creating a love potion visited her one evening. She told him it could be done, but he would have to forfeit his firstborn child to her as payment. Angry because of the deal that was offered him, he attacked the woman and she was killed (some say he impaled her on a cypress tree). Since that day, the ghost of the witch has been seen and heard here.

Locals say sightings of the spirit were so prevalent that at one point an angry mob burned the witch's old shack down, hoping this would banish her from the area. It did not work. A visit to this location just may get you your first glimpse of this phantom.

## Hyder Bridge—Lula, Georgia

The story of Blind Suzie has been attached to this bridge for quite some time, even though she most likely lived in a completely different area. Hyder Bridge, also known as the Lula Covered Bridge, was built in 1915 and now spans a tributary of Oak Grove Creek. It's listed on the National Register of Historic Places (and has a plaque that will give you more background information concerning the bridge), but is mostly known because of the associated ghost of Blind Suzie.

Suzie was known far and wide during the days of prohibition for selling a mean batch of moonshine, and she did business right on her front porch. She would hide jugs of the liquor under her skirts as she sat in an old chair and sell the stuff to locals who had the money to buy it. When she passed away, folks began claiming to see the old woman on the bridge. Those who have seen the apparition say she stands on the span and simply ignores those who pass by. People also claim that, even when she isn't visible, she is still there; apparently animals won't cross the old bridge and those who visit the historic site say they can hear the sounds of an old woman humming.

## CCC Road—Rome, Georgia

What if there wasn't one haunted bridge, but seven of them instead? And what if it was the bridge itself that was one of the ghosts? According to students at nearby Berry College, if you drive along CCC Road—known locally as Seven Bridges Road—you will count seven bridges during the drive. But then, if you turn around and drive back the way you came, you will only count six. One bridge will have mysteriously disappeared. Is it an optical illusion? Some say yes. Others have a more ghostly reason for this disparity.

It seems that a young man committed suicide along this stretch of road in 1993 (the death was reported by local news sources) and his apparition has been seen standing in the vicinity of where his body was found. Many believe it is his mischievous spirit that's having fun with people driving along here. Either way, check out this bizarre stretch of road—and while you're at it, you may want to visit nearby Berry College. With numerous ghost stories associated with the campus, it would be a great way to top off a fun, haunted excursion.

## Hooper Springs Park Bridge—Soda Springs, Idaho

The tiny bridge in the middle of this city park seems to be the center of attention for a strange type of haunting. While most people visit this recreational area to sample the natural soda water that flows here—or to simply enjoy the playground, picnic areas, and nature—there are those who say the park is crawling with a particular type of ghost: Shadow People. Dark, shadowlike spirits have been witnessed on the bridge, walking through the trees, and even frolicking in the playground. Strangely, this unique paranormal event has been seen during the day, as well as the evening.

While nobody believes the entities are evil, it does seem to be a phenomenon that spooks those who see the ghosts in action. If you plan to check out the area for yourself, pack a picnic and visit the site a couple hours before nightfall. Most parks close at sunset, so your best shot at seeing these ghosts is going to be the period leading up to (and including) dusk. Take along a camera with low light capabilities and you just might get something interesting.

## Rock Creek Bridge—Twin Falls, Idaho

Okay, so this bridge is technically not around anymore, but the remnants are said to still be visible in the Twin Falls river canyon area. When it was standing, locals referred to the structure as the Singing Bridge, and it was known for a particularly bizarre haunting. While the bridge is now gone, the haunting is certainly still around.

The ghost story involves what is known as the Devil's Henchman. Supposedly, if you make the climb into the canyon area beneath where the bridge stood, you will find some rock stairs that lead to an area where you will find a series of carved faces in the rock. These faces are supposed to represent a series of people who were abducted—and presumably murdered—from the region. To make the tale even a bit more frightening, it's said that the angry spirit here does not like visitors. As you get closer to the carvings, you will begin to hear voices in the wind and get an uneasy feeling in the pit of your stomach (sometimes a symptom of high electromagnetic fields).

If you get online and Google the bridge, you can read several first-hand accounts about visiting the Singing Bridge, but it seems that people never quite find the faces. They get too scared en route and usually turn back.

## Seven Gates to Hell—Collinsville, Illinois

Along Lebanon Road, on the outskirts of the town of Collinsville, is a series of seven bridges. Some are quite small—railroad-style spans—but they are all there for those who wish to find them. Of course, you will be wanting to cross them at night since that is the time specified in order to open a gate to Hell. That's right, according to legend, if you manage to cross all seven bridges in a row, with your vehicle crossing the seventh bridge at exactly midnight, a portal to the hoary netherworld will appear. You will know you have achieved this feat when you suddenly notice the presence of hellhounds with glowing eyes that immediately pursue you. Sounds great, right?

So how did this area manage to get this particular feature? Many say it started with an old house standing in the area that was once the site of a grisly murder. Some say it was a family member who went insane and killed everyone; some say it was a ritualistic slaying by Satanic cult members. Since that horrific act, the house has been used for rituals and cult activities—and as a result, the portal to Hell was created.

Now if this sounds like the kind of supernatural bridge you'd like to skip, I should mention that the worst thing that will probably happen while you are attempting to cross the Seven Gates to Hell is encountering a slew of rowdy teenagers.

## Hell's Gate—Clay County, Indiana

Finding this bizarre location is the first challenge if you plan to visit this spot. You need to leave the town of Diamond and head south on North Rock Run Church Road. The bridge in question is actually a set of train tracks crossing over a tunnel. You will know the tunnel instantly; it is covered with graffiti and red paint, and it smells terrible. Sometimes this tunnel is closed off to the public; sometimes it is open to drive through. If it is closed, respect the law and check it out from afar. If it's open ...

According to legend, a terrible train accident happened at this crossing—one that killed dozens of people. This act, according to ghost enthusiasts, opened up a gate to Hell. In order for you to open this portal, you are supposed to stop at the entrance to the tunnel, flash your lights three times, then drive through the tunnel three times, stopping in the center on the third pass. If you then turn off your vehicle and pay attention, strange things are supposed to happen.

Some say the paint will disappear off the walls and everything turns a bloody red. Some say dark figures will pass the vehicle and disembodied voices will begin to wail. Even others tell of a tall specter that will approach your car and attempt to enter and get you. Sounds fun, right?

## Main Street Bridge—Fort Wayne, Indiana

Sometimes when you get an explanation for a haunting it is more ridiculous than the haunting itself. Such is the case with the famous Lady in White, who is said to walk Main Street in the town of Fort Wayne. The *Fort Wayne Gazette* documented the first sighting of this spirit in 1883. According to the article, witnesses watched this woman walk along until she suddenly disappeared in the middle of the bridge. Many assumed the lady had leaped from the bridge, so a search was made with nobody found below. Not long after this, the same ghost was seen in a horse-drawn carriage crossing the bridge—and everything disappeared at the exact same spot.

The mystery became a local sensation until the paper then reported that the haunting had been debunked. They sited a local man by the name of Johnny Hanna as the culprit. Apparently he had a lantern with shapes cut into the sides and he was shining these shapes to appear on the bridge. So the paper would have us believe that a small crowd—and, later, a pair of police officers—would mistake a light shining from a lantern for an apparition (once with a spectral horse and carriage). Right…

Of course, even if you buy the explanation for this whole incident, it doesn't explain why people still see the spirit of the Lady in White walking along Main Street and occasionally hear the sounds of a female voice on the wind.

## Lake City Bridge—Lake City, Iowa

This awesome specimen is a prime example of the famous James B. Marsh "Rainbow Bridge" design. Known by various names—Raccoon River Bridge, Rainbow Bridge, and the aforementioned Lake City Bridge for starters—this location would make a great day trip, or perhaps even an overnight stay.

Closed to automobile traffic, this bridge is the centerpiece of Rainbow Park. So when you're not staking out the structure for ghostly activity, you can take advantage of fishing in the Raccoon River; camping in a small, primitive campsite; and picnicking beneath the trees. Besides, the haunting of this particular place is a bit, well, odd.

Apparently, if you place an unopened chocolate bar on the bridge and leave it there, it will be consumed by a hungry spirit. It's said that when you check on the candy you will find the wrapper to be unopened, but the chocolate will be gone. Weird? A bit. Oddly enough, there doesn't seem to be any other ghostly activity here. So, if you plan to check out the dead chocoholic, you may want to take along that nice picnic basket and your camping gear. Might as well make a fun trip of the whole affair.

## Atlas Avenue Bridge—Shell Rock, Iowa

Tales of Satan's Hollow Bridge have been whispered around campfires in Iowa for quite a few years now—unfortunately, the tale seems to vary with each telling and the fare seems more suited to a horror movie than a story based on any kind of facts. That said, those who have had an experience at this site say it was quite frightening.

The story goes that, if you make the trip beneath the bridge, you will experience more and more of the uncanny as you near Shell Rock River (and I should mention that messing around under *any* bridge at night is probably a bit dangerous, so you may want to skip it altogether). So, what happens exactly? Well, it seems that a mysterious cult used to perform rituals at this location, and because of this, people now hear chants/voices, feel eyes on them as they near the river, and sometimes even see the odd sight of multiple ghostly figures shrouded in white. I presume this means they are wearing robes. (They're members of a cult, remember?)

While the entire story smacks of urban legend, it's worth your time to Google some of the stories about Satan's Hollow Bridge. Some are quite frightening. Just use caution if you decide to test the legend for yourself.

## Roseman Covered Bridge—Winterset, Iowa

This bridge is a movie star of sorts—a book and, subsequently, a movie were written about it titled *The Bridges of Madison County*, and it even appeared in the film. Dating back to 1883, this gorgeous structure crosses Middle River and is listed on the National Register of Historic Places. It should come as no wonder that a place with this much history is now regarded as haunted.

There are two tales concerning the strange activity that happens at this spot, and both pretty much end up the same way. The first version tells of a young man who was courting a local girl. He went to meet her one day and found her father, along with an angry mob, waiting for him. He fled on horseback and was pursued to the bridge. When the posse got there they saw the horse, now riderless, exiting the far side of the structure, but the young man had disappeared. The second edition of the tale is pretty much the same, only the young man escaped from the local prison and there was an actual exchange of gunfire in the bridge before the man disappeared. Either way, it's said the soul of the missing man is now trapped in the bridge somehow.

People have told of feeling frighteningly cold spots in the center of the bridge, hearing the sounds of horses/gunshots, and even glimpsing what looks like the apparition of a young man.

## Heartbeat Bridge—Ellicott City, Maryland

Located over a creek just off Bonnie Branch Road, this spot is a well-known oddity in the area. Most locals know—and will happily tell the story—of how a jealous husband once cut out his wife's heart and tossed it into the creek. So does she now haunt the bridge over the creek? Well, maybe…

It's sort of hard to quantify this tale as a haunting since nobody sees a ghost or hears a ghost or experiences anything of any sort that we typically think of as being part of a ghost story. So, what does happen here? Well, if you walk across the bridge (watch out for traffic), you will supposedly feel a vibration after a few moments—a steady, pulsing vibration that is said to be the dead woman's heart. This heartbeat is so strong it's said that, if you park your vehicle on the bridge (much safer than walking), you will feel it inside your car.

While no one seems to put much stock in the validity of the killing, everyone will tell you the experience is quite real. It's so popular in Ellicott City that it's listed on the official website of the town.

## Old Highway 94 Bridge—Jefferson City, Missouri

Located on the outskirts of town, this bridge has such a bizarre assortment of legends associated with it that it deserves to be in no other chapter than here. The most common tale involves the spirit of an old fellow nicknamed Ofie. Ofie apparently likes to pretend he's been hit by passing cars and then disappear when you search for him. Since there is no great description of Ofie, it's best you treat all the people on this bridge as real and attempt to *not* hit them.

Another well-known yarn about this bridge involves a creature that stalks the area. Said creature stalks people who park to make out and is often seen peering from roadside foliage. Need more stories? Great! There is also a mysterious light that has been seen on Old 94 approaching the bridge and, if that's still not enough, good old-fashioned ghosts are known to haunt the bridge, too. The story goes that the spirits were once a family who supported the Union in the American Civil War. Others didn't appreciate their political views, so they hung the family. They are now seen here, as well as heard.

The most commonly experienced activity at the bridge seems to be the sounds of children crying and screaming. Interestingly, in 2013 a couple skulls were found in the vicinity of the bridge.

## Highway 200 Bridge—Trout Creek, Montana

So, you've read passages in this book about scary monsters, ghosts lingering in various areas, and glowing balls of light scooting along the road. Here is something altogether different—unidentified flying objects (UFO's). Sightings of flying saucers at this bridge were discovered in a very unique way—a savvy online individual using Google Earth spotted what looked like a spaceship hovering over the Trout Creek area. Not only does the craft in question appear to be a flying saucer, it also seems to feature an alien hanging out the ship's sunroof. Yep, you read that right.

Apparently, searching for alien aircraft via Google Earth is now quite the popular hobby, and today folks consider this bridge a UFO hotspot. If you want to take a break from visiting haunted bridges, you might want to head out to Trout Creek and do some UFO watching. Just be warned that, statistically, your odds of seeing a flying saucer are even lower than the odds of seeing/hearing a ghost. Good luck with your hunt.

## Old US Highway 34 Bridge—Grand Island, Nebraska

Everything about this bridge is interesting. Open only to pedestrian traffic these days, this bridge used to be a busy thoroughfare in the area. Now it has a motel on one end and is a tourist attraction for everyone who enjoys chasing down a scary story. Known as Witch's Bridge, people have been telling campfire tales about this span for decades. The most common tale being, of course, about the witch. It's said she lived in a house nearby and would perform rituals of all sorts along the Platte River, including human sacrifice. When the locals had enough of her, they burned her home down. Some say she was in it; some say she cursed them and fled. Now the ghosts of her victims, as well as other evil things she unleashed, haunt the bridge.

A second story is told about a woman and child who were on the bridge when an explosion shook the structure. She dropped her child into the water below, where he/she drowned. The woman's ghost is now supposed to be seen on the bridge, too. With a couple scary stories being told it's probably no surprise that Witch's Bridge has become a bit of a local dare.

Visitors to the span say that cars die for no reason, disembodied voices can be heard, and frightening apparitions have been seen. At least one source I spoke to about this bridge said that it is now owned by the motel there (a Motel 6 at the time I'm writing this), so you may consider staying in the hotel and asking for a guided tour.

## Clinton Road Bridge—West Milford, New Jersey

Where to begin? When a stretch of road has as many legends, sightings, and bizarre happenings as this rural landmark, it's difficult to tell a coherent tale. I guess we should start with the bridge. The ghost of a young boy seems to haunt the structure, and he has a peculiar way of letting you know he is still around…

If you look into the water below the structure, you will notice it's quite shiny. This is because of the coins that people have thrown there. It's said that if you toss in a penny, the ghost boy will toss it back. Some say this happens immediately, some say if you return later the coin will be lying on the road where you were standing. Sounds interesting enough, right? But visiting this specter is usually just the tip of the iceberg for those legend tripping along Clinton Road.

Other prime stops on Clinton Road include an old iron smelter known for ghosts (often called a "Druidic temple" by locals), Cross Castle (a dilapidated set of ruins that once was a manor and is now said to be the site of Satanic rituals and horrific creatures), and the site where a bizarre ice man was found. Toss in sightings of a ghost car, UFO's, hellhounds, and apparitions walking the road, and you have one interesting stretch of road.

## Teeter's Bridge—Mount Pleasant, North Carolina

The stretch of County Road 1132 (CR1132) between Mount Pleasant Road South and Barrier Georgeville Road has a small bridge known to locals as Teeter's Bridge. It's named after a farmer who lived nearby named John Teeter, but this isn't the original bridge to stand at this site. The older incarnation was a small wooden span that was known for flooding.

It was during a night of heavy rains that folks say a young mom was on her way home with her baby when she had an accident. With the low visibility and water on the road, she drove off the side of the bridge. She and her baby were drowned in the waters of Dutch Buffalo Creek. These days the bridge is a modern, concrete affair, but ghostly activity still occurs at the site, albeit in a very odd way.

Apparently there is a large stone with the name Furr emblazoned on it that's near the bridge, and when there's a night like the evening the woman died (rain), this stone bleeds. Some say other rocks along the streambed weep blood, too. It's an odd memorial to an accident that may or may not have actually happened. If this doesn't seem quite your cup of tea, others have noted paranormal activity at the bridge, too, including screams and a dark figure that's often seen roaming around.

## Seven Bridges Road—Rocky Mount, North Carolina

Rather than being a listing about a single spooky bridge, this passage is about seven bridges along one road and a strange story. It's said that if you drive along NC-97 East from Rocky Mount to the small hamlet of Leggett, you will count seven bridges. But if you then turn around and drive back, you will only count six bridges. One has disappeared.

It's an odd tale that a lot of people know in the area. Some say it is simply an optical illusion, some say it happens because of a much darker reason. The belief is that this road is an evil area that likes to mess with people's heads. Over the years, there have been a lot of accidents on this stretch—and some have pointed out that several bodies were found on this road (they are believed to be the victims of a serial killer that plagued the region and was responsible for ten missing women).

Of course there's no way to know for yourself if the bridge disappears or not, unless you make the trip yourself. Considering the stories about the road, though, you may not want to stop and look for the missing span.

## Dean Road Bridge—Vermilion, Ohio

Dating back to 1898, this historic structure was updated with some renovations in 1992, but it still looks pretty rough. Looming over the Vermilion River, this location has drawn people to participate in a rather odd, but not entirely unique, event. It's said that if you park on the bridge, turn off your car, and wait for a bit, you will begin to feel and hear what sounds like a heartbeat. It will grow stronger and stronger, accompanied by the sensation that something is approaching your vehicle, until it suddenly stops.

Some say the heartbeat is nothing more than a factory nearby, but the story persists. Especially since the bridge is part of a larger urban legend known as Dean's Hollow. The hollow is a well-known excursion for the legend tripper, featuring additional spooky spots around the area. In addition to Heartbeat Bridge, you also get a creature that's rumored to have massacred people, a bridge on Morse Road that has a ghost (someone was reputedly hung there), and a crazy cult that torments people who wander there. Since I don't recommend parking your car on a bridge, you may want to test the heartbeat out nearby on the side of the road. Otherwise, keep a lookout for monsters and cultists.

## Crooked River High Bridge—Jefferson County, Oregon

Looming almost three hundred feet above the canyon below, this picturesque bridge was constructed in 1926 and is accompanied by the Peter Skene Ogden State Park just to the south. With the canyon and nearby trails (as well as the park), this area is known for its abundance of outdoor activities. It's known for something a bit odder as well…

People say there are places in the world where the veil between our reality and the past/future is thin. These places are known for bizarre acts taking place that are often mistaken for ghosts. It has been supposed, however, that you are not seeing a haunting, but are looking through the veil at events happening in some other time or reality. Deep stuff, huh? This area around the canyon is said to be one of these places.

The stretch of road leading up to the bridge (US Highway 97) is encounter central with eyewitnesses telling of spectral people walking the road, the spirits of cows and other animals appearing, and people experiencing the sensation of losing consciousness. Native Americans knew of this phenomenon and consider the canyon itself to be a place of import. Go for a hike there and see if you can catch a glimpse through the veil for yourself.

## Gudgeonville Covered Bridge—Girard, Pennsylvania

Spanning Elk Creek, this bridge dates back to 1868 and is listed on the National Register of Historic Places. It was the victim of two arsonists in 2008 and has been replaced with a temporary bridge until it can be figured out how to best permanently replace the structure. The bridge itself was quite a tourist attraction, but when you add in the haunted folklore that pervades the area, it becomes a ghost hunter's dream trip.

The bridge is said to be haunted by a very strange soul—a dead mule that locals have dubbed Gudgeon. It's said the mule died after receiving a beating from its owner (though some say it died of a heart attack because of music playing on a passing barge) and can now be heard clomping across the span. In addition to this, the bridge is also supposed to have been used for hangings back in the day. Now witnesses say you can catch glimpses of bodies swinging underneath and hear disembodied voices pleading for help/crying.

If you're up for a little exploring, you may want to check out another spot close by called Devil's Backbone. It's a sheer cliff that has claimed a few lives over the years and some have seen the apparitions of two young girls there.

## Skyhill Road Bridge—Mahoning Township, Pennsylvania

It's hard to separate the stories about this bridge and the surrounding area in general. Dubbed Zombieland by the locals, this entire region is teeming with legends, fables, and folktales. The bridge over Coffee Run was recently replaced with a brand-new, clean version—but the old structure still exists, too. The graffiti-covered old span is known alternately as Frankenstein's Bridge and Puerto Rican Bridge.

The story goes that if you find your name written here (presumably with spray paint) you will soon die. Rumors of the ghost of a young boy, who is said to have committed suicide here, are also discussed. On a sad note, the body of a young girl was actually found dead here in 2000; she was raped, stabbed to death, and then found close by. Perhaps the spirit is hers?

A trip to Zombieland is dangerous for real world reasons (people drinking, violence, etc.), but perhaps a good day trip could be made to explore all the folklore. Other stories about the area include the former site of the Blood House where a witch once lived, the legend of the Green Man and a glowing tombstone, and the Killing Fields where the sounds of screams and gunshots are heard, accompanied by misty apparitions roaming around. Spooky stuff, right?

## T-Bridge—Gaffney, South Carolina

Located along Montgomery Street in downtown Gaffney, this bridge crosses the Norfolk Southern Railway (and, yes, it is actually called T-Bridge). It dates back to 1919, though it was completely renovated in the 1970s, and it is known for a couple odd events of a ghostly nature. The first involves running across the bridge on foot; if you do this, a phantom car will appear with no driver and pursue you. Fortunately, it reputedly disappears just before actually hitting you. The second odd happening involves the appearance of an apparition of an old woman carrying a basket full of flowers. You're supposed to stand at the bridge with your eyes closed for ten minutes. When you open them, she will be standing there staring at you. Much like the ghost car, when you approach the old woman she simply disappears before you make contact.

I could find no information about whether or not this bridge has a sidewalk or pedestrian crossing. If it does allow for pedestrians, give the legends a whirl. If not, it's probably not worth the risk running across the bridge.

## Green Elm Cemetery Bridge—Chico, Texas

Falling somewhere between the story of La Llorona and legends concerning the Bean Sidhe (banshee), the tale of the screaming woman on the West Fork Trinity River is now a renowned yarn that gets a good telling around campfires in these parts. Mostly due to a first person account by G. E. Francis (who was ninety-two years old at the time), this old bridge is still drawing folks who love a good, spooky place.

The bridge is located about one thousand feet from Green Elm Cemetery and is quite dilapidated, but this doesn't matter much; the entity is seen on the river itself. According to Francis, when he and three others encountered the thing in 1948, they were taking a nature break by the road when they heard a horrible scream echoing from the river. Upon investigation, the four of them saw a Mexican woman in a white dress floating down the river in midair over the water. She appeared to be in anguish and trapped by the water itself—almost as if she was bound to the river. She floated downstream, over the bridge, and continued until she was out of sight. And she was wailing the entire time; they are purported to be the sounds of a horrible nightmare. Others have seen the specter since, though it does seem to be a sporadic kind of event.

## FM 1960 Overpass—Humble, Texas

This basic concrete span over a set of train tracks has had quite the haunted history attributed to it. The story goes that when the road and overpass were built, a cemetery had to be moved to accommodate construction. Some say it was moved properly, some say only part was moved, but they shifted all the headstones (in other words, some people are still buried beneath the road). Whichever is true, this act angered the spirits and a portal to the otherworld was opened. Now the entire area is said to be ridden with evil entities that frighten people, do malevolent deeds, and occasionally appear to the unwary wanderer. Several businesses near the overpass are said to be infested with the presence of these demons—and several others are now closed because of supposed appearances by these things.

A quick Google search will bring you a lot more lore about this crazy legend, as well as lots of fan pages about the spot. I did manage to find one paranormal investigation that happened at the overpass; results were inconclusive, but there were a couple nightmarish electronic voice phenomena (EVPs) recorded at the site.

## Troll Bridge—Marshall, Texas

Everything about this tale is odd. Let's start with the bridge itself; it's located sitting in the woods, apparently crossing nothing. It's inaccessible by car, so you have to park on Sue Belle Lake Road and then hike into the woods to find the place. It's also quite dilapidated, but that's okay. You won't have to walk on it.

You want to be searching the area for a bizarre spirit named Myrtle Mary. Said to be a woman who died in a railroad accident, this strange woman from Marshall was found dead wearing clothes made out of goatskins. There's apparently something quite popular with goats in this part of Texas (just read about the two Goat Man bridges detailed in this book). Now the goat ghost of Myrtle Mary patrols the woods around Troll Bridge.

Oh yeah, did I mention the bridge is called Troll Bridge? Once again, this has to do with goats. The story of the Three Billy Goats Gruff involves a trio of goats crossing a bridge that has a troll underneath it. With our story we get the bridge and the goats (well, their skins anyway), but there's no trolls. Unless you talk to kids who live in the area. They are all too ready to take the spooky spec-ter of Myrtle Mary and trade her out for a troll. Whatever is in these woods, it's said to growl and scream during the night. Good luck with this one.

## East Ashley Road Bridge—San Antonio, Texas

Known locally as Devil's Bridge, this concrete bridge over the San Antonio River has a few urban legends attached to it. It's said the entire area around the bridge is a portal into Hell—or at least an-other dimension/world where dark, evil things reside. The phe-nomenon here doesn't happen all the time, but when it does you know it. Everything will suddenly go dark—so dark that you can't see any light around you—and the horrifying sounds of screams/ moans will fill the air. At that moment you are said to be in Hell. But don't freak out. The portal will close as quick as it opens and you will be left, once again, in this world.

Strangely, if you are outside of the portal area, you are still sup-posed to see the massive, lightless area. One witness stated that he tossed a stone into the darkness and never heard it land (some have supposed that something caught it within the darkness). It's an odd tale, but those who have had an experience on the bridge, or near it, say the ordeal is terrifying. What's scary about the prospect of being trapped in a dark world of the dead and demonic?

## K Street Bridge—Washington, DC

Being a complex set of bridges, ramps, and roads, it's much harder to pinpoint a location along this thoroughfare for the ghost enthusiast to visit. Suffice it to say, any of the roads leading up to the area will probably be good for catching a glimpse of this bizarre spirit.

Since the mid-1800s, people have claimed to see a headless apparition galloping across the bridge. So, technically, it's two ghosts: The headless man and the horse. He's been seen on adjacent roads, too, so don't sweat trying to figure out which span over Rock Creek and the Potomac Parkway is the correct one.

Since the sightings for this particular apparition have been rather sporadic over the centuries, your odds are rather low for seeing him anyway. Maybe you should use this bridge as a jumping off point for a neat haunted exploration of the area. There are two more haunted bridges in Washington, DC, and many other spooky places that are known for their ghosts.

## Sock Road Bridge—Lowell, Wisconsin

The current span along Sock Road is the second bridge to exist at this spot. The first was torn down years ago—and it, of course, was the one associated with the haunting. But like most haunted bridges, the tale (and possibly the ghost) has carried over to the new incarnation here. So who haunts this spot? Good question. Absolutely nobody knows. What's more, it may not even be a ghost based on the activity at this location.

Locals say if you drive your car onto the bridge and park, the rails of the bridge will begin to drip blood. So, haunted rails or a living bridge that bleeds? Again, nobody knows. The story, however, is quite well known, and it usually draws area teens to the bridge to test the legend and get into trouble. There's no reason I can think of that would make rails bleed, so you will simply have to visit this place for yourself to test the tale.

# CONCLUSION

So you've made it this far. You've read an entire book about bridges with ghosts, bridges with monsters, and bridges with spooky lights crossing them. What have you learned?

Hopefully it has become clear just how delicate the division between fact and fiction is. What is one person's legend is another person's paranormal experience. In the world of the supernatural, anything is possible and everything is debatable. So, like many things in life, anything you take away from these varied tales is dependent entirely upon you.

The fact that you would even read a book about this subject indicates that you are at least willing to accept the possibility that many of the tales told in these pages could be true. And for me that is enough. As for you … well …

You probably need to check out the bridges for yourself. At least the ones that are listed in your area. Just heed my advice: Be careful, take along a friend, and keep an open mind. You never know what you're going to find.

# BRIDGE LISTING BY STATE

(Alphabetical by City)

## Alabama

Pleasant Hill Road Bridge—Attalla, Alabama / 59

Lovelady Bridge—Camp Hill, Alabama / 60

Refuge Bridge—Clanton, Alabama / 230

Oakachoy Covered Bridge—Coosa County, Alabama / 5

Old Dora Train Trestle—Dora, Alabama / 6

Second Creek Bridge—Elgin, Alabama / 115

Kayo Road Bridge—Hartselle, Alabama / 61

Camax Mill Bridge—Jasper, Alabama / 155

Alamuchee-Bellamy Covered Bridge—Livingston, Alabama / 7

Bayview Bridge—Mulga, Alabama / 156

Choctawhatchee Bridge—Newton, Alabama / 8

Salem-Shotwell Covered Bridge—Opelika, Alabama / 157

Kali Oka Road Bridge—Saraland, Alabama / 62

## Alaska

CR & NW Bridge—Chitina, Alaska / 203

## Arizona

Jones Park Bridge—Arizona City, Arizona / 157

London Bridge—Lake Havasu, Arizona / 83

## Arkansas

Cotter Bridge—Cotter, Arkansas / 204

Tilly Willy Bridge—Fayetteville, Arkansas / 129

Billy's Bridge—Mena, Arkansas / 183

Wolf Bayou Bridge—Pulaski County, Arkansas / 62

Des Arc Bridge—Springfield, Arkansas / 84

## California

Mill Creek Bridge—Bakersfield, California / 158

Santa Margarita Bridge—Fallbrook, California / 205

Creek Park Bridge—La Mirada, California / 230

Mossdale Bridge—Lathrop, California / 41

Creek Road Bridge—Ojai, California / 130

Colorado Street Bridge—Pasadena, California / 42

Santa Ana River Bridge—Riverside, California / 131

Golden Gate Bridge—San Francisco, California / 85

Arbuckle Creek Bridge—Lorida, Florida / 232

Bellamy Bridge—Marianna, Florida / 184

Train Trestle Bridge—Melbourne, Florida / 208

Mathers Bridge—Merritt Island, Florida / 88

Little Econ River Bridge—Orange County, Florida / 185

Bob Graham Sunshine Skyway Bridge—Tampa Bay, Florida / 116

John's Pass Bridge—Treasure Island/Madeira Beach, Florida / 88

Griffin Road Bridge—Wauchula, Florida / 159

## Georgia

Muckalee Creek Bridge—Americus, Georgia / 159

Metropolitan Avenue Bridge—Atlanta, Georgia / 117

Oconee Cemetery Bridge—Athens, Georgia / 89

Lickskillet Railroad Bridge—Austell, Georgia / 90

Euharlee Covered Bridge—Bartow County, Georgia / 8

Hardin Bridge—Bartow County, Georgia / 186

White's Bridge—Colquitt, Georgia / 209

Alcovy Trestle Bridge—Covington, Georgia / 160

Parrish Mill Covered Bridge—Emanuel County, Georgia / 161

Whitesville Road Bridge—Gainesville, Georgia / 64

Holland Road Bridge—Hawkinsville, Georgia / 134

Hyder Bridge—Lula, Georgia / 233

Camp Creek Trestle—McDonough, Georgia / 210

Carver Mill Bridge—Pickens County, Georgia / 210

CCC Road—Rome, Georgia / 233

Concord Covered Bridge—Smyrna, Georgia / 31

Highway 341 Bridge—Surrency, Georgia / 187

Withlacoochee River Bridge—Valdosta, Georgia / 161

Stovall Mill Covered Bridge—White County, Georgia / 64

## Hawaii

16th Avenue Bridge—Kaimuki, Hawaii / 118

Seven Bridges Trail—Manoa Valley, Hawaii / 90

## Idaho

River Road Bridge—Caldwell, Idaho / 9

Plaza Road Bridge—Emmett, Idaho / 65

Lower Loon Creek Bridge—Salmon-Challis National Forest, Idaho / 162

Hooper Springs Park Bridge—Soda Springs, Idaho / 234

Rock Creek Bridge—Twin Falls, Idaho / 235

## Illinois

Blood's Point Bridge—Belvidere, Illinois / 135

Black Jack Road Bridge—Canton, Illinois / 66

Clark Street Bridge—Chicago, Illinois / 91

Bear Creek Bridge—Christian County, Illinois / 136

Airtight Bridge—Coles County, Illinois / 163

Seven Gates to Hell—Collinsville, Illinois / 235

Old Post Road Bridge—Crete, Illinois / 164

Old Train Bridge—DePue, Illinois / 92

Love Ford Bridge—Jasper County, Illinois / 45

Lakey's Creek Bridge—McLeansboro, Illinois / 164

Cedar Creek Bridge—Monmouth, Illinois / 32

Zingg Road Bridge—Millstadt, Illinois / 10

Sugar Creek Bridge—New Holland, Illinois / 10

Cataract Covered Bridge—Owen County, Illinois / 11

## Indiana

Ceylon Covered Bridge—Adams County, Indiana / 137

Avon Bridge—Avon, Indiana / 211

Tunnel Mill Road Bridge—Charlestown, Indiana / 212

Hell's Gate—Clay County, Indiana / 236

Old Railroad Bridge—Columbus, Indiana / 137

Main Street Bridge—Fort Wayne, Indiana / 237

Edna Collins Bridge—Greencastle, Indiana / 118

Williams Covered Bridge—Lawrence County, Indiana / 93

5th Road Bridge—Marshall County, Indiana / 138

Brooks Bridge—Martin County, Indiana / 46

Hamilton Road Bridge—Mulberry, Indiana / 119

Norris Ford Covered Bridge—Rush County, Indiana / 165

Old Kankakee River Bridge—San Pierre, Indiana / 139

Cannonball Bridge—Vincennes, Indiana / 12

## Iowa

Kate Shelley High Bridge—Boone, Iowa / 93

Matsell Bridge—Central City, Iowa / 32

Lake City Bridge—Lake City, Iowa / 238

Skunk River Bridge—Metz, Iowa / 140

Giblin Bridge—Mount Pleasant, Iowa / 13

Atlas Avenue Bridge—Shell Rock, Iowa / 238

Bannwell Bridge—Webster County, Iowa / 13

Roseman Covered Bridge—Winterset, Iowa / 239

## Kansas

Coon Creek Bridge—Barnes, Kansas / 188

Rocky Ford Bridge—Emporia, Kansas / 166

Cedar Creek Bridge—Olathe, Kansas / 67

Jester's Creek Bridge—Valley Center, Kansas / 188

## Kentucky

Colville Covered Bridge—Bourbon County, Kentucky / 212

Old Richardsville Road Bridge—Bowling Green, Kentucky / 33

Child's Creek Bridge—Closplint, Kentucky / 120

Cumberland Falls Bridge—Corbin, Kentucky / 47

Taylorsville Road Trestle—Fisherville, Kentucky / 140

Cody Road RR Bridge—Independence, Kentucky / 141

Carter Bridge—Oak Grove, Kentucky / 167

Crybaby Bridge—Shelbyville, Kentucky / 67

Middle Bridge—Warren County, Kentucky / 213

Ghost Bridge—Winchester, Kentucky / 214

## Louisiana

Bayou Tortue Road Bridge—Broussard, Louisiana / 168
Boeuf River Bridge—Fiske Union, Louisiana / 189
Charles Burr Lane Bridge—Opelousas, Louisiana / 120
Marland's Bridge—Sunset, Louisiana / 168

## Maine

Goose River Bridge—Rockport, Maine / 94

## Maryland

Governor's Bridge—Bowie, Maryland / 68
Acton Lane Bridge—Charles County, Maryland / 142
Heartbeat Bridge—Ellicott City, Maryland / 240
Jericho Covered Bridge—Jerusalem, Maryland / 14
Walnut Tree Bridge—Millington, Maryland / 69
Lottsford Road Bridge—Mitchellville, Maryland / 70
Roop's Mill Road Bridge—Westminster, Maryland / 70

## Massachusetts

Eunice Williams Covered Bridge—Greenfield, Massachusetts / 95

## Michigan

Adrian Train Trestle—Adrian, Michigan / 214
Rogue River Bridge—Algoma Township, Michigan / 169
Trowbridge Road Bridge—Bloomfield, Michigan / 48
Crawford Road Bridge—Cass City, Michigan / 215

Puttygut Bridge—China Township, Michigan / 190

Dice Road Bridge—Hemlock, Michigan / 143

Fallasburg Bridge—Lowell, Michigan / 48

Mackinac Bridge—Mackinaw City, Michigan / 49

Old Stronach Bridge—Manistee, Michigan / 96

Oakwood Avenue Bridge—Owosso, Michigan / 50

White's Bridge—Smyrna, Michigan / 15

## Minnesota

Washington Avenue Bridge—Minneapolis, Minnesota / 50

Arcola High Bridge—Stillwater, Minnesota / 190

## Mississippi

I-10 Bridge—Gautier, Mississippi / 144

Burnt Bridge—Hattiesburg, Mississippi / 96

Stuckey's Bridge—Meridian, Mississippi / 16

## Missouri

Nine Mile Bridge—Auxvasse, Missouri / 170

Upper Blackwell Road Bridge—Blackwell, Missouri / 121

Katy Trail Bridge—Columbia, Missouri / 97

Rosemary Road Bridge—Florence, Missouri / 171

Enoch Knob Bridge—Franklin County, Missouri / 144

Old Highway 94 Bridge—Jefferson City, Missouri / 241

Wainwright Bridge—Jefferson City, Missouri / 34

George Brett Bridge—Kansas City, Missouri / 216

Riverside Bridge—Ozark, Missouri / 98

Union Covered Bridge—Paris, Missouri / 35

Crybaby Bridge—Senath, Missouri / 71

Phelps Grove Park Bridge—Springfield, Missouri / 217

## Montana

Highway 200 Bridge—Trout Creek, Montana / 241

## Nebraska

Darr Bridge—Cherry County, Nebraska / 99

Old US Highway 34 Bridge—Grand Island, Nebraska / 242

295 Avenue Bridge—Platte Center, Nebraska / 99

Road C Bridge—Spring Ranch, Nebraska / 16

## Nevada

Mike O'Callaghan-Pat Tillman Memorial Bridge—Clark County, Nevada / 51

## New Hampshire

Ledyard Bridge—Hanover, New Hampshire / 100

Black Bridge—Nashua, New Hampshire / 217

## New Jersey

Combs Hollow Road Bridge—Mendham, New Jersey / 218

Old Mine Road Bridge—Warren County, New Jersey / 101

Clinton Road Bridge—West Milford, New Jersey / 243

Highway 130 Bridge—Westville, New Jersey / 145

## New Mexico

US 70 Bridge—Las Cruces, New Mexico / 72

## New York

Mill Street Bridge—Angola, New York / 219

Fiddler's Bridge—Clinton Corners, New York / 220

Stone Arch Bridge—Kenoza Lake, New York / 171

Brooklyn Bridge—New York City, New York / 52

Troy Country Club Road Bridge—Troy, New York / 220

## North Carolina

Craven Street Bridge—Asheville, North Carolina / 221

Zealandia Bridge—Asheville, North Carolina / 53

Broad River Bridge—Caroleen, North Carolina / 122

Chair Factory Road Bridge—Columbus County, North Carolina / 172

Sally's Bridge—Concord, North Carolina / 73

Lydia's Bridge—Jamestown, North Carolina / 122

Teeter's Bridge—Mount Pleasant, North Carolina / 244

Tar River Bridge—Pitt County, North Carolina / 146

Pisgah Covered Bridge—Randolph County, North Carolina / 17

Seven Bridges Road—Rocky Mount, North Carolina / 244

Bostian Train Bridge—Statesboro, North Carolina / 101

Morphus Bridge—Wendell, North Carolina / 191

Hardison Mill Creek Bridge—Williamston, North Carolina / 73

## North Dakota

White Lady Bridge—Leroy, North Dakota / 53

## Ohio

Greely Chapel Road Bridge—Allen County, Ohio / 173

Tindall Bridge—Ballville, Ohio / 173

Walhalla Road Bridge—Columbus, Ohio / 18

Ridge Avenue Bridge—Dayton, Ohio / 174

Garfield Park Bridge—Garfield Heights, Ohio / 102

Blue Bridge—Huron County, Ohio / 192

Johnston Covered Bridge—Lancaster, Ohio / 54

Fought Road Bridge—Lindsey, Ohio / 192

Maud Hughes Road Bridge—Middletown, Ohio / 193

Stonelick Covered Bridge—Milford, Ohio / 19

Newton Falls Covered Bridge—Newton Falls, Ohio / 74

Everett Covered Bridge—Peninsula, Ohio / 103

Muskingum River Bridge—Philo, Ohio / 75

Brubaker Covered Bridge—Preble County, Ohio / 222

Egypt Road Bridge—Salem, Ohio / 75

Bloody Bridge—Spencerville, Ohio / 175

Hansley Road Bridge—Sugar Grove, Ohio / 194

Gibbs Road Bridge—Sylvania, Ohio / 19

Dean Road Bridge—Vermilion, Ohio / 245

Dug Hill Road Bridge—Wapakoneta, Ohio / 222

Rogue's Hollow Bridge—Wayne County, Ohio / 76

McConnell's Mill Covered Bridge—Lawrence County, Pennsylvania / 224

Sheard's Mill Covered Bridge—Haycock Township, Pennsylvania / 147

Hogback Road Bridge—Hermitage, Pennsylvania / 197

Hunsecker's Mill Covered Bridge—Lancaster, Pennsylvania / 37

Lehigh Canal Trestle—Lehighton, Pennsylvania / 55

Skyhill Road Bridge—Mahoning Township, Pennsylvania / 247

Crum Creek Bridge—Media, Pennsylvania / 107

Long Lane Bridge—Millersville, Pennsylvania / 21

Slateford Trestle—Mount Bethel, Pennsylvania / 225

Roaring Spring Bridge—Roaring Spring, Pennsylvania / 21

St. John's Road Bridge—Slippery Rock, Pennsylvania / 198

Van Sant Covered Bridge—Solebury Township, Pennsylvania / 77

## Rhode Island

Colt State Park Bridge—Bristol, Rhode Island / 108

Moosup River Bridge—Moosup Valley, Rhode Island / 108

Main Street Bridge—Pawtucket, Rhode Island / 123

## South Carolina

High Shoals Road Bridge—Anderson, South Carolina / 78

Cherokee Falls Bridge—Blacksburg, South Carolina / 22

Gervais Street Bridge—Columbia, South Carolina / 124

Lee Roy's Bridge—Gaffney, South Carolina / 175

T-Bridge—Gaffney, South Carolina / 248

Poinsett Bridge—Greenville County, South Carolina / 23

Devenger Road Bridge—Greer, South Carolina / 38

Wateree River Bridge—Laurens County, South Carolina / 125

Three Bridges Road—Powdersville, South Carolina / 176

Tyger River Bridge—Union, South Carolina / 79

## South Dakota

West 26th Street Bridge—Sioux Falls, South Dakota / 125

## Tennessee

Drummond Bridge—Briceville, Tennessee / 24

Crazy George's Bridge—Dry Hollow, Tennessee / 198

Hanniwal Bridge—Elkton, Tennessee / 79

Watauga River Bridge—Elizabethton, Tennessee / 177

Scarce Creek Road Bridge—Lexington, Tennessee / 24

Burnt Mill Bridge—Scott County, Tennessee / 177

## Texas

Clear Fork River Bridge—Anson, Texas / 25

River Legacy Park Bridge—Arlington, Texas / 199

Joppa Bridge—Burnet County, Texas / 148

Green Elm Cemetery Bridge—Chico, Texas / 249

Mud Creek Bridge—DeKalb, Texas / 80

Old Alton Bridge—Denton, Texas / 149

Moeller Road Bridge—Electra, Texas / 178

Broadway Avenue Bridge—Haltom City, Texas / 179

Pecan Creek Bridge—Hamilton, Texas / 150

Langham Creek Bridge—Houston, Texas / 109

Old Greenhouse Road Bridge—Houston, Texas / 199

FM 1960 Overpass—Humble, Texas / 249

Brushy Creek Bridge—Hutto, Texas / 38

Old Buffalo Lake Bridge—Iowa Park, Texas / 179

Troll Bridge—Marshall, Texas / 250

Maxdale Road Bridge—Maxdale, Texas / 56

Sarah Jane Road Bridge—Port Neches, Texas / 80

Old Leakey Road Bridge—Rio Frio, Texas / 180

Donkey Lady Bridge—San Antonio, Texas / 150

East Ashley Road Bridge—San Antonio, Texas / 251

Thompson Island Bridge—San Marcos, Texas / 109

Woman Hollering Creek Bridge—Schertz, Texas / 151

Barnes Bridge—Sunnyvale, Texas / 39

Wellington Lane Bridge—Wichita Falls, Texas / 151

## Utah

Bear River Bridge—Bear River City, Utah / 81

Provo Canyon Road Bridge—Bridal Veil Falls, Utah / 126

Mountain Meadows Trail Bridge—St. George, Utah / 110

## Vermont

Float Bridge Road Bridge—Castleton, Vermont / 111

Long Bridge—Newport, Vermont / 152

## Wisconsin

Jay Road Bridge—Boltonville, Wisconsin / 127

Dyreson Road Bridge—Dunn, Wisconsin / 181

Weary Road Bridge—Evansville, Wisconsin / 227

Sock Road Bridge—Lowell, Wisconsin / 252

Grant Park Covered Bridge—Milwaukee, Wisconsin / 201

## Wyoming

Shoshone River Bridge—Cedar Mountain, Wyoming / 154

Fort Laramie Bridge—Goshen County, Wyoming / 113

# BIBLIOGRAPHY/REFERENCES

While most of my research was done through the use of the Internet and by contacting people directly (when possible), there are a few books that I referenced directly for this book for various reasons. All are worth a read in and of themselves. Here they are for your convenience:

Cox, Dale. *The Ghost of Bellamy Bridge: 10 Ghosts & Monsters from Jackson County, Florida.* Bascom, FL: Old Kitchen Books, 2012.

Holland, Jeffrey Scott, and Mark Moran. *Weird Kentucky.* New York: Sterling, 2008.

Lake, Matt, and Mark Moran. *Weird Pennsylvania.* New York: Sterling, 2009.

Price, Charles Edwin, and Richard Blaustein. *Haints, Witches, and Boogers: Tales From Upper East Tennessee.* Winston-Salem, NC: John F. Blair Publishing, 1992.

Steiger, Brad. *Real Ghosts, Restless Spirits, and Haunted Places.* Canton, MI: Visible Ink Press, 2003.

Wolfe, Thomas. *Look Homeward, Angel.* New York: Scribner, 2006.

## To Write the Author

If you wish to contact the author or would like more information about this book, please write to the author in care of Llewellyn Worldwide, and we will forward your request. Both the author and publisher appreciate hearing from you and learning of your enjoyment of this book and how it has helped you. Llewellyn Worldwide cannot guarantee that every letter written to the author can be answered, but all will be forwarded. Please write to:

Rich Newman
℅ Llewellyn Worldwide
2143 Wooddale Drive
Woodbury, MN 55125-2989

Please enclose a self-addressed stamped envelope for reply,
or $1.00 to cover costs. If outside the U.S.A., enclose
an international postal reply coupon.